Impressed and Incised Ceramics

17.95

IMPRESSED AND INCISED CERAMICS

Coll Minogue

A & C Black · London

Gentle Breeze · Florida

First published in Great Britain 1996
A & C Black (Publishers) Limited
35 Bedford Row
London WC1R 4JH

ISBN 0–7136–3957–1

© Coll Minogue 1996

Published simultaneously in the USA by
Gentle Breeze Publishing.
P.O. Box 1484, Oviedo, Florida 32765

ISBN 0-9650786-2-0

A CIP catalogue record for this book is available
from the British Library.

Filmset by August Filmsetting, St Helens
Printed in Hong Kong by Wing King Tong Co, Ltd

Acknowledgements

I am indebted to all those who have
provided both illustrations and
information for this book. Without their
generosity of spirit it could not exist.

Cover illustrations
front Casket by Lara Scobie (UK), 1994, 15 × 14 cm.
Several different techniques were used to create the
range of textures on this piece. Porcelain.
Photograph by John McKenzie.

back Detail of a dish by Siddig El'nigoumi (Sudan/
UK). Sgraffito decoration. Earthenware. Press
moulded. *Photograph by Coll Minogue.*

Frontispiece Three Dishes (detail) by Jane Hamlyn
(UK). Low relief pattern on interior of bases created
by rolling textured wallpapers onto the slabs from
which they were formed. *Photograph by Nick
Broomhead.*

Contents

Health and Safety Advice

Some of the processes described in this book, in particular those in the chapters on Incising, involve working with clay in a dry or semi-dry state. When there is a possibility of dust being created when working with clay and other ceramic materials, a dust mask or respirator, covering the nose and mouth and fitted with the appropriate recommended safety standard filter(s), should be worn.

Introduction

Pressing into a soft surface to leave an impression, or incising a mark, are satisfying and fundamental actions. Creating footprints in damp sand, or drawing or writing in it with a stick, gives a certain pleasure even though we realise that these marks are transitory and will be washed away by the incoming tide.

Leaving a mark in a material which is capable of retaining that mark is a different experience. We are somehow attracted to an area of wet cement which has just been levelled off. There is a desire to leave a hand print, a footprint or another personal expression – our initials and the date – knowing that when the

Shell impression.

Li Ding (Tripod), China, Western Zhou Dynasty, 1027–771 BC, 14 cm/h × 14 cm/dia.
Earthenware. Impressed pattern (probably matting). *Glasgow Museums: The Burrell Collection (38/37)*.

cement dries, they will be made permanent. Then there is clay with its unique combination of properties – plasticity; the ability to accept and retain impressions; and the manner in which it is transformed by the action of heat. Making marks in soft clay, knowing that when dried and fired it will last indefinitely, has attracted people to this medium throughout history.

These unique properties have been exploited since objects were first fashioned from clay. Potters have always used things from their environment to embellish clay surfaces. Prehistoric vessels have impressions of shells, bones and fingernails. There are also impressions created by manmade objects, some specifically made for the purpose (stamps, roulettes), while others were adapted for use. Today, many of these same techniques continue to be used by ceramicists worldwide. In some ways this is surprising since there are now more options for decorating clay surfaces available than ever before. However the appeal of making marks directly into clay endures, and the evidence of what it is possible to achieve using these basic techniques, visible in pots from throughout history, offers constant inspiration and encouragement.

There is of course a far greater variety of manmade objects available to today's ceramicists. But just as the objects used by prehistoric makers to texture clay surfaces reflected life around them, the materials used for the same purpose by artists today reflect the time in which we live. This point is illustrated throughout the book by the inventive and creative uses to which found objects are put by contemporary ceramicists. For some, the impressed or incised marks they make are regarded as decoration, their purpose being to embellish and enhance a form, to add interest, or to create a texture which will be enlivened as a result of the firing technique used. For others, the impressing and/or incising are part of the build up of the overall form and are integral to it. For yet others, the act of impressing or incising actually alters the form, and is therefore a fundamental part of the making process. There are also artists for whom the act of impressing or incising (or the objects used to carry out these processes) are in themselves part of the overall artistic statement.

In his book, *Warren Mackenzie – An American Potter*, David Lewis writes,

> The tools MacKenzie uses for engraving, fluting, or carving the surfaces of pots are mostly homemade from wood, bamboo, metal strapping, or rubber. He is continually looking for curious objects that he can use to shape or alter the surface of pots. Many come from junk shops, hardware stores, or the kitchen appliance sections of supermarkets. Picking through his toolbox, I found among his standard tools a cheese cutter, a wire whisk for beating eggs, a cheese grater, a nutmeg grater, a zigzag pie crust cutter, a bradawl, a plumber's rasp, a narrow-gauge wire mesh, butter paddles with different patterns, heavy-treaded wheels from a child's toy truck, and a bed caster with triangular indentations filled into its surface.

This description is probably typical of many of those whose work is described in this book, and of the objects to be found in their toolboxes.

The two terms, 'impress' and 'incise', encompass between them almost all of the methods of decoration which it is possible to carry out in clay between the stages from soft to leatherhard. In order to accommodate the very wide range of work being produced, all of which could be broadly described as impressed or incised, I have chosen ten chapter headings for the part dealing with Impressed techniques and four chapter headings for the part on Incised techniques. In the two chapters which make up Part Three, there are accounts of the personal approaches of two artists who work in clay, using techniques which could loosely be described as 'impressed' and 'incised'.

In deciding on the different chapters to include, it became clear that the divisions were in some instances blurred, in that it was not always possible to draw clear distinctions between the techniques being discussed. For example, when a length of cord is rolled across a clay surface to create an impressed texture, it could perhaps be described as a roulette. However, I have placed this technique in a chapter of its own, rather than in the chapter on roulettes. Similarly in the part on Incising, there are definite grey areas between chapter headings; for instance between Incising and Carving. Having referred to dictionary definitions of the different terms involved, in the end I have had to rely on my own discretion when deciding where to place the work of individual ceramicists or information on particular techniques.

Scattered throughout the book are illustrations of pots from different countries and different periods in the history and prehistory of pottery. All of these pieces illustrate various examples of decorating techniques and surface treatments which can be described as impressed or incised. My choice of historical examples has been heavily influenced by my own preferences: pots of the Japanese Jomon Period; Neolithic and Early Bronze Age pottery in Britain and Ireland; pottery of the Early Cycladic Period, from the Cyclades, and Bronze Age Cypriot pottery. Of these, Jomon pottery is referred to most frequently. Apart from personal preference, the reason is that this was an extremely long period (extending from approximately 10,000 BC or even earlier, to 250 BC), during which many of the decorating techniques with which this book is concerned, were used extensively, individual techniques coming to prominence at different stages within the period.

For me, one of the most rewarding aspects of writing this book has been the necessary research into, and observation of, a very wide range of prehistoric, historic and contemporary works in clay. I began to see impressed and incised marks on pieces where I had never noticed them before. This encouraged me to look beyond forms, carefully study surface textures, and to try to figure out how various marks were created and textural effects achieved. Clay, perhaps better than any other material, allows us to trace back from the fired work to establish how it was constructed and decorated.

Understanding how an effect was achieved on vessels made thousands of years ago assists us to identify with those pieces to a certain extent, and perhaps also with the potters who made them. If this book has the effect of whetting readers' appetites for closer observation and a greater understanding of the work of both our predecessors and today's ceramicists, (and perhaps resulting from this, acts as a stimulus for experimentation in, and development of, some of the techniques described), then I will consider that it has succeeded in its primary aims.

Part 1

Impressed

Jar, China, Han Dynasty, 206 BC–AD 220, 23.5/h 33 cm/dia. Impressed decoration (a fired clay stamp was probably used). Earthenware. *Glasgow Museums: The Burrell Collection (38/43).*

Chapter One
Impressions Using Natural and Manmade Objects

NATURAL OBJECTS

Impressions made by natural objects have been part of pottery-making since the very start of its history. Fingertip marks were probably at first accidental, left as a result of the techniques used to form clay into objects, such as pinching and coiling. Evidence of hand modelling including fingertip and fingernail marks has been found on fragments of figurines found at Dolni Vestonice, in the former Czechoslovakia, dating from *c.*24,000 BC (according to radiocarbon dating). However, on later pottery from different countries, distinct fingertip impressions are to be found, placed regularly and clearly, decorating and creating a texture on the surface of pots.

History

In Japan the production of pottery may have begun as early as 10,000 BC and marks the start of what is known as the Jomon period. Some of the earliest shards show raised ridges of clay which were finger pinched. Initially such ridges probably resulted from the forming process used i.e. narrow slabs or flattened coils of clay were pinched together to join them, thus producing narrow ridges. On other shards this 'linear relief', as it is known, appears to have been formed by applying strips of clay, and may have been for purely decorative purposes.

Shards showing ridges forming a hatched pattern have been found, as well as patterns where the ridges have been pinched to form wavy lines. After 'linear relief', the next type of surface marks to appear on pottery in Japan were fingernail markings. These are arranged in bands parallel to the rim, vertically in rows, or in patterns running diagonally on the surface. (So-called 'nail markings' which appear later on during the Jomon period were apparently made using the end of a split bamboo stick.) Shell impressing was another method of surface decoration used on Jomon pots.

Examples of fingertip impressions can also be seen on Neolithic and Bronze Age British pottery and are especially common on pottery of the second millennium BC. They appear as large oval impressions and may be paired, resulting in raised cordons, or arranged to create more complex patterns. Fingernail impressions were also used extensively on pottery of this period. By pressing a fingernail into soft clay a distinct crescent shape was achieved. When impressed in pairs, fingernail impressions produced a splayed V shape, which when arranged in rows formed herringbone patterns. Examples of complex patterns have been found, where alternate areas of herringbone pattern comprised of vertical and horizontal rows of fingernail impressions, are bordered by incised lines. Decoration was also carried out on pots of this period using bird or animal bones. The end of a small bone was repeatedly pressed into soft clay to create an overall pattern. The shape of the impression could be changed by altering the angle at which the tip of the bone was pressed into the clay. Evidence of the use of another natural object for the purposes of decorating a clay surface is to be seen on Beaker pottery of this period (a distinctive pottery style which spread to Britain from Europe at the beginning of the second millennium BC). Shell edge impressions, creating all over decoration, are to be seen on pottery from the coastal sites of Northern Britain.

Another example of the use of natural objects to impress patterns on pots is the impressions of leaves on the bases of some of the conical cups made by the Keros-Syros culture (c.2,700–2,200 BC) in the Cycladic Islands in the Aegean Sea. While these impressions may have been picked up accidentally when the pots were left to dry prior to firing, it is also possible that the impressions were made on purpose to ornament the pots which are otherwise undecorated. The case for the latter possibility is strengthened by the fact that the impressions are placed symmetrically and the leaves were pressed into the bases sufficiently to result in deep and very clear impressions.

Technique

When natural objects such as leaves, seed pods, shells, grasses etc. are pressed into soft clay and then removed, we are left with fossil-like images. The knowledge that once the clay is fired, the image, delicate as it may appear, will be captured and rendered permanent, has a certain fascination, just as the fossil laid down millions of years ago never ceases to amaze. However, using natural objects to decorate pots is more than a case of just recording the impression of a leaf or a blade of grass. The successful incorporation of marks left by embedding natural objects in a clay surface, involves several factors and considerations: selecting objects with shapes and textures which are appropriate for the pots you make, and how the textures will be affected by glazes or firing effects, markings or colours. It is important to begin by having an overall concept of the effects you want to achieve, whether arranging the objects to make up a pattern, or using the impressed marks left by natural objects as part of a decorative scheme, combined with other decorating techniques.

Current practices

Many potters working today use natural objects to decorate their work. One such potter is Micki Schloessingk (UK), who frequently uses shell impressions in her work which is wood-fired and salt-glazed. In many instances shells are used to decorate the slab dishes she makes. Micki writes:

> I enjoy shell impressing as it is incredibly simple. I use the shell to press into the firm, but not quite leatherhard clay, before I apply slip to the pots. I also use the shells sometimes to stand the pots on instead of alumina wads. The shell disintegrates leaving a fine fossil-like impression in the clay. I use my thumbnail to incise lines in the clay to also add to the decoration. The very fines lines of the shell pick up the salt glaze and leave a vivid imprint, each shell has a different pattern.

Shells are also impressed into other work, including thrown vases and bottle forms. The effect achieved in wood-fired, salt-

Slab Dish by Micki Schloessingk, (UK) 1994, 10 cm × 10 cm. Impressed shell decoration. Wood-fired, salt glaze. *Photograph by Graham Mathews.*

glazed work tends to be in some way quieter, less glossy, than when other fuels (gas or oil) are used. These effects perfectly complement Micki's work. The use of unobstructive shell markings is in keeping with the overall effect; the forms, colours and textures, creating a harmonious whole.

American potter Jack Troy uses bisque-fired stamps (made by impressing natural objects into soft clay) to texture the surfaces of his porcelain and stoneware pots. Objects used include Savoy cabbage leaves and burdock leaves. In addition to leaf patterns, Jack has also used fossils and rope-textured bisque-fired stamps to impress surfaces. Regarding possible influences on his work, Jack comments

Jomon pottery interests me more than any other. Being unaccompanied by any contemporaneous verbal explication, it exudes all the power and delicacy necessary to make us realise that our perceptions of beauty probably haven't evolved all that much in 10,000 years.

Much of Jack's work is fired in an Anagama kiln. He describes the effects of this type of firing on his work as follows: 'The firing process – incorporating direct flame to enhance what I have consciously formed – assists my intentions by accentuating the most subtle variations in surface depth. On a good day.'

Rather than pressing natural objects into clay and then removing them, or making stamps from them which are in turn pressed into clay, some artists view the impressing as integral to their artistic statement. The object is left pressed into the clay, either to be burned away during the firing, or to be altered following a low-temperature firing, the fragments remaining embedded in the fired clay. During the late 1970s and early 1980s Hungarian artist Imré Schrammel made a series of reliefs which were imprints of dead birds he found. After firing, all that

Slab by Jack Troy (USA), 1990, 40 × 33 × 4 cm. Textured with bisque-fired stamp impressed with Savoy cabbage leaf. Porcelain. Anagama fired. Natural ash glaze.

remained were the skeleton and a ghostly impression of the bird. These reliefs were exhibited and given titles which made statements about mankind's attitude to and treatment of nature.

MANMADE OBJECTS

Almost as early as humans made marks using natural objects to embellish clay surfaces, they went a step further and began using objects which they had shaped or altered in some way for this purpose.

History

Throughout prehistoric and historic pottery there is ample evidence of potters having cut or carved wood, bone and horn to create objects suitable for making marks in clay. On shards of some of the earliest pottery to be found in Japan, there are marks which appear to have been made by rolling and pressing a squarish stick (probably about the size and shape of a matchstick) continuously on the clay surface. A later development of this technique was to carve designs in short

lengths of stick which were rolled on the clay surface to impress a pattern (see chapter on roulettes).

Examples of objects made from bone being used as tools to decorate pots are the combs used to impress patterns on Neolithic and Bronze Age pottery. These combs were curved, dentated shapes, usually polished rib or scapula fragments. When such an implement was pressed into the surface of leatherhard clay, the result was a line of small, regular-shaped impressions, either square or rectangular. This technique was used extensively on beakers either to create zones of decoration (see photograph on page 62), or in bands around the pot completely covering the exterior surface, with as many as 2,000 to 5,000 individual comb tooth impressions on each pot. Another technique for making surface marks on pottery of this period involved the use of pointed implements made from either wood or bone. The point was pressed at an angle into the surface of leatherhard clay and then dragged slightly along the surface as it was being withdrawn (a technique referred to by archaeologists as 'stab and drag'). This produced narrow triangular impressions, which were often arranged diagonally in alternate rows, to create a pattern of regular chevrons.

Current practices

One aspect of my own work which is wood-fired involves the use of a variety of

Left
Beaker – Perthshire, Scotland, *c.*2450–1600 BC, 13.4 cm/h, 14.7 cm/w. The decoration of 12 rows of chevrons was created by inserting a pointed tool or spatula into the surface at an angle to form narrow triangular impressions. © *The Trustees of the National Museums of Scotland 1996 (unreg.).*

blocks and lengths of wood, both in the forming and to create textures on slabs of clay, some of which are made into dishes. The following is a description of the technique I use in making these dishes.

Once a slab of clay has been rolled out on a very finely woven piece of cloth, it is cut to the required shape. Then working on one edge at a time, the edges of the fabric are folded over to cover the edges of the slab. By running a finger along each edge through the fabric, the sharp angle made by cutting is softened. The slab is then covered with another piece of cloth. Using the edge of a piece of wood, the end of a wooden modelling tool or anything else which is suitable, the slab is beaten to create impressed marks. Beating through cloth results in softer marks. With the cloth still in place, a block of wood or other material used as a former, is put in position on the slab, which is then turned upside down to rest on the former. A rubber kidney is rubbed over the backing cloth to gradually push the slab down over the former, giving definition to the dish shape. The backing cloth is removed and the slab allowed to dry for a time. Then, lengths cut from a coil of clay are applied as feet to the dish. It is important that the dish is not allowed to get too dry while the former is still in place, as this could result in cracking. On the other hand, if the dish is turned the right way up and the former removed too soon, the slab will probably sag and flatten out, so careful monitoring of the drying process is required. On other dishes made in this way, the impressions made by the former (or in some cases two or more formers) are used as the basis for decorative schemes which might include impressing shells or stamps, combing etc.

An aspect of woodfiring which attracts many potters is the fact that during the firing clay is 'decorated' with flame and

Above
Slab dish by Coll Minogue, 1995, 15 cm ×
15 cm. Impressed marks. Wood-fired
stoneware. *Photograph by Paul Adair.*

Sculptural form by Paul Soldner (USA),
67 cm/h × 91 cm/w × 56 cm/d. Wheel
thrown and altered. Shoe sole and fabric
imprints. Applied slips. Low temperature salt-
fired.

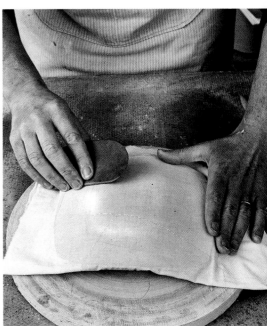

Having rolled out a slab of clay, a cloth is placed over it, an impressed pattern is created and then a former is put in position.

A rubber kidney is used to ease the slab into a dish shape over the former.

Lengths cut from a coil of clay are attached to form feet.

Three slab dishes, prior to firing (detail).
Photographs by Paul Adair.

Juglet, Tell-el-Yahudiyeh Ware, Egypt, Second Intermediate period, 1650–1551 BC 11.2 cm/h 5.8 cm/dia. Pattern of impressed zigzag lines, probably created with a square toothed comb. Thrown. Attached base. *Ashmolean Museum Oxford (1888.268).*

fly ash. The duration of the firing, the design of the kiln, and the clay body used, are all contributing factors to the effects achieved. The textured patterns created in the manner described above, are quietly accentuated during the woodfiring. The marks do not distract attention from the flashings of colour and deposits of fly ash and the texture created by the marks adds depth and interest to the fired clay surface.

American ceramic artist Paul Soldner has made extensive use of manmade textures in his sculptural forms. The textural effects are created by impressing found objects into the clay as the pieces are worked on. On this aspect of his work and his reason for using these textures Paul comments as follows:

It is partly because I like the idea that as artists, we have always reflected in some way, life around us in our work. What more surrounds us than the clothes we wear, the automobile tyre tread, plastic crates etc. . . . and clay, better than any other medium, accurately takes a mirror image of any object pressed into it. Beyond this I use the organic qualities of clay and fire to add to whatever I pressed into the clay intuitively.

In addition to pressing found objects into the clay surface, Paul likes 'to make templates from panel board, which reflect images from magazines. Sometimes they are only advertising, other times they can be from photos I take of people.' These templates are then pressed into the clay surface to create imprints. Many of Paul's pieces are thrown and then altered – cut, dropped, stamped on, objects pressed in

etc. Later, slips are applied before the work is low-temperature salt-fired. Writing of Paul's work in *Ceramic Review* (No. 109 – Jan/Feb 1988) Dave Roberts wrote:

Soldner's command and orchestration of a wide range of variables in decoration and firing enhance his articulation of the plasticity and responsiveness of clay in the incisive record of human mark making activity. These objects carry layers of meaning and reveal a masterly synthesis of process and control.

Vladimir Tsivin, an artist who lives in St. Petersburg, is known for the torso pieces he creates, which are reminiscent of ancient sculpture, especially Greek and Roman. One of the techniques used by Tsivin to achieve subtle effects suggestive of textiles or drapery is to press ribbed rubber matting into the clay slabs from which his sculptures are constructed. The result is a surface with shallow, impressed, parallel lines. There is no modelling of details – the form of a torso, just hinted at beneath the 'textile' covering, seems to be pressing outwards creating a remarkable effect.

The work of both Vladimir Tsivin and Paul Soldner clearly demonstrates how the marking processes used in the creation of powerful sculptural ceramic pieces can involve the use of simple, everyday, found objects. The inventive use of found manmade objects is not confined to this chapter. Throughout the following chapters, there are several examples of the creative use made of found manmade objects by ceramicists producing a very wide range of work.

Chapter Two
Cord

The pressing and rolling of a short length of twisted cord on a soft clay surface is perhaps the most common use of cord to decorate pots. However throughout the history of pottery, cord has been used in other ways to make impressed marks – pressed in bands around a pot; coiled around sticks which were then rolled across the surface; wrapped around paddles, which when used to beat a pot into shape, left an impressed cord pattern; braided or plaited to make different patterns, which created a variety of impressed marks when rolled on clay.

History

Jomon – the name given to the period from approximately 10,000 BC to 250 BC in Japan, means 'cord marked' or 'cord pattern'. Throughout the period, cord was used in one way or another to leave impressed marks on the surface of pots. Techniques varied from simply winding a string over the top of the thumb and pressing it into the clay, or pressing cord using the fingertips, to very complex effects achieved by twisting strands of cords together, coiling cords around sticks and rolling them on the clay surface, or knotting cords to create specific decorative effects. Single strands or 2 or 4 strands were either twisted or braided to achieve a very wide variety of textural effects. Twisted cord technique was also used to create herringbone patterns, by alternating bands of left diagonal and right diagonal impressions. The cord wrapped stick technique was used to make several different patterns including fishnet, woodgrain and chain. The fishnet effect was achieved by winding string diagonally around a slender stick, leaving spaces between the rows of string.

Fragment of a jar, from Hokkaido, Japan, Jomon Period, 33 cm/h × 17.8 cm/w. Bands of impressed cord decoration. © *The Trustees of the National Museums of Scotland 1996 (1914.139).*

Beaker, West Lothian, Scotland, c.2450–1600 BC, 14.6 cm/h. Decorated all over with impressions made with twisted cord, including three lines on the interior of the rim. © *The Trustees of the National Museums of Scotland 1996 (EG 47).*

Another piece of string was then wound in the opposite direction, criss crossing the first string. When this stick was then rolled on clay, a distinct fishnet impression was created. By knotting string, either in single or double knots, and then rolling it on clay, other effects were achieved. Cord markings were often restricted to particular areas on a pot and used as part of an overall decorative pattern, in combination with techniques such as incising, carving and applied decoration, to create some extremely complex and elaborate patterns.

Cord decoration in different forms was also used on Neolithic 'Beakers' (see Chapter 1). One of these, known as 'All over Cord' decoration, which as the name implies, consisted of encircling lines of impressed twisted cord markings, usually covering the entire exterior of the beaker and sometimes continuing within the rim (see photograph above). Short lengths of cord were also impressed to create repetitive herringbone, chevron or lattice patterns.

Another technique used on food vessels and urns of this period was whipped cord decoration. This involved wrapping twisted cord, either around itself, or another core material, to make a short, fat length which was then pressed into soft clay, to produce segmented impressions, also known as 'maggots' (see photograph on page 49).

Technique

Before more elaborate methods of decorating with cord are attempted, probably the most direct technique to try is that of rolling a short length of twisted cord across a clay surface. As regards the type of cord to use, a smooth cord with an interesting texture is probably best to try. Avoid cords which have loose strands. Ships chandlers usually have a wide range of cords in various sizes, made up of different numbers of strands. Nylon cord is probably best, as it is more durable than those made from natural materials/fibres. The ends of the length of cord must be secured before use, otherwise they will fray. If the cord is of a nylon type, the ends can be sealed by melting them to form blobs. Alternatively, the ends can be bound by winding thread or thin cord or twine, very tightly around them.

After throwing a pot, in order to create a smooth, flat surface suitable for decorating, it is best to remove any pronounced throwing rings by using a rib. Allow the pot to dry for a while. Next dip the cord in water so that it will not stick to the surface during use. A length of cord no longer than 10 or 12 cm is probably the most manageable size. With the wheel revolving slowly or alternatively walking around the pot, slowly roll the length of cord around the circumference – starting with the cord at the tips of the fingers, then rolling it towards the palm, along the full length of the fingers. Make sure that the wall of the pot is supported on the inside using your other hand. Having created one band of texture around the pot, it is best to overlap the next band, rather than try to match up exactly with the first one. Overlapping in this way will help to create a continuous effect and to avoid pronounced seam lines. If the cord becomes clogged with clay, rinse it out in water before continuing. This type of decoration can be carried out on clay at various stages of dryness with varying degrees of success; the softer the clay the deeper the impression which can be achieved. Some potters do rolled cord decoration on freshly thrown pots, others allow the surface to stiffen to a soft leatherhard state before proceeding further. The drier the clay surface the shallower and less pronounced the impression it is possible to achieve. Rolled cord is a very versatile decorating technique; as the length of cord used is flexible, it can be used on clay surfaces whether concave (the interiors of bowls), convex (the exteriors of bulbous forms) or flat.

Current practices

Wood-fire potter Svend Bayer (UK) uses rolled cord to decorate much of his work, including large garden pots, up to 66 cm high by 66 cm wide. These pots are made by first throwing the bottom bowl-shaped section, and once this has stiffened sufficiently, large coils are added which are then thrown. Once the rim has been completed, the pot is allowed to dry for a time. Then a short length of twisted cord is rolled around the pot, with the bands of decoration overlapping each time. A large area is left undecorated towards the bottom of the pot. Next, partly pulled handles are attached to the pot, the pulling is completed and the ends attached to form large strap handles. A narrow roulette is used to decorate the

Plate by Svend Bayer (UK). Rolled cord and impressed stamp decoration. Wood-fired stoneware. Natural ash glaze.

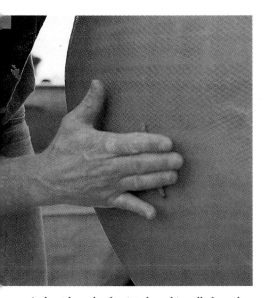

A short length of twisted cord is rolled on the surface of the pot, creating an impressed pattern. *Photograph by Coll Minogue.*

Section of the completed pot showing cord impressed surface, handle with rouletted texture and applied pad of clay with stamped impression. *Photograph by Coll Minogue.*

handles and is continued to cover the areas where they are joined to the pot. Finally, circular pads, formed by flattening small balls of clay, are attached to the body of the pot, in positions in line with the handles and midway between them. A stamp with a linear pattern is pressed into each pad to complete the decoration. Svend's pots are fired in a 250 cubic foot (7 m³), crossdraught, wood-fired kiln. On the fired pots, the cord textured areas create an interest and contrast with the areas which have been left undecorated. The flame marks and ash deposits resulting from wood firing, often highlight the texture of the cord marking and make it more pronounced. Svend's work is influenced by the traditional pottery of South East Asia, an area in which he travelled, prior to establishing his workshop in Devon in 1975.

Another wood-fire potter, Jonathan Garratt (UK), also frequently uses rolled cord decoration on his terracotta garden

pots. One of the decorative patterns he uses is achieved as follows. Having covered approximately two-thirds of the exterior surface of a shallow planter with cord decoration, a number of lines are made by running a narrow roulette vertically down the pot from top to base, thus dividing the cord decoration into areas. Small pellets of clay are applied at the top of each rouletted line, to complete the decoration. (See photograph on page 26.)

Rolled cord decoration can be the initial stage in inlaid decoration, as in the work of Japanese potter Tatsuzo Shimaoka. Slip is brushed into the impressions left by rolling a length of cord on the surface of a pot. When the slip has dried, it is carefully scraped off to reveal the pattern created by the slip remaining in the impressions made by the cord. This technique is particularly effective when the colour of the slip contrasts with that of the background clay body.

In common with many of the

Planter with rolled cord and rouletted decoration (prior to firing) by Jonathan Garratt.

decorating techniques described in this book, the textured surface created by rolling cord can be particularly effective when covered with a coloured transparent or semi-transparent glaze, or one which displays quite a variation between thick and thin applications. The bowl by American potter Warren MacKenzie (see photograph below), with rectangular areas of rolled cord decoration, bordered by incised lines and glazed in a tenmoku glaze – pooling to a dark colour in the depressions of the pattern and breaking to rust on the raised areas – clearly illustrates this.

Bowl by Warren MacKenzie (USA). Rolled cord and incised decoration.

Chapter Three
Stamps

In the context of this book the term 'to stamp' means to press an object, usually fairly small in scale, into soft clay to leave an impression.

History

Stamped decoration is to be found on pots made in the Cycladic Islands, in the Aegean Sea, by the Keros-Syros culture (*c.*2700–2200 BC). Stamps were used particularly on the so-called 'frying pans'. These are generally in the form of a disc, with a shallow rim round it (thus the resemblance to a frying pan). They also have short 'handles' which differ in shape from pot to pot. It is not clear what function these pots served, but from the very elaborately decorated surfaces, it is thought that they were in some sense special and may have been used in rituals of some kind. Those found on the island of Syros are of a more developed style than examples from other islands. Three different decorative motifs occur on this pottery – small triangles arranged in alternate rows so that a zig-zag pattern is formed, concentric circles, and spirals which are often linked together (running spirals). The stamps used to make these impressed designs were probably made of wood. Stamped decoration is often combined with incised patterns. The surface of the pots is usually highly polished and black or red in colour (see photograph below).

Examples are in existence of pots with repeated stamped decoration, dating from the Meroitic Period in Egypt (*c.*300 BC – AD 400). These pots were wheel-thrown 'fine' wares – bowls, vases and cups, thrown very thinly. Typically, the stamped impression, made with a small ornamental stamp, was repeated in bands around the pot. The walls of the pots are so thin that the pressing in of the stamp, left a distinct raised area on the inside surface. Pots are of a pale yellow/buff colour or a warm pink tone.

Stamps were also used extensively as a method of decoration in Anglo-Saxon pottery of the 5th–9th centuries. These stamps were made from a variety of materials including animal antlers, teeth

'Frying Pan', Cycladic Islands in the Aegean Sea, Keros-Syros culture, *c.*2700–2200 BC 18.5 cm/dia. Impressed stamp decoration. *Ashmolean Museum Oxford (1971.842).*

and bones, clay and perhaps also wood. Parts of jewellery were also used to create stamped impressions during this period. Designs for stamps vary from simple cross, circle, square and triangular shapes, to more elaborate geometric patterns – circles within circles, grid patterns, crescents and cartwheels. The use of stamped ornament on Anglo-Saxon pottery is generally combined with other methods of decoration, such as linear grooves (see photograph below). Several different designs of stamps were often used on the same pot.

During the United Silla period in Korea (AD 668 – 935) stamped decoration was widely used. Large covered funerary urns and other vessels such as jars, bowls and vases made from unglazed stoneware had elaborate stamped decoration. Frequently used motifs include triangles and concentric circles. Later, during the Koryo Dynasty (AD 935–1392), repeated stamped impressions were used as the basis for inlaid patterns. (See Chapter 14 on Inlay.) Stamps were made from bamboo, wood, clay and sometimes metal stamps were used. This technique continued in use in the Yi Dynasty, which followed on from the Koryo Dynasty.

Stamped decoration was also widely used on Mediaeval English pottery. In some examples a stamp was pressed directly into the surface of a pot, while on others, the stamp was impressed into pads of clay applied to the pot. Stamps were often used in combination with other decorative features, such as strips of clay applied vertically or diagonally, which were then stamped.

Technique

Almost anything can be used as a stamp to press into and leave an impression in clay. The size of the object being used is generally the limiting factor (impressing clay using large areas of texture is dealt with in a subsequent chapter). Here, I am primarily concerned with small-scale stamps and in particular self-made stamps.

A number of different materials can be used to make stamps, including clay, plaster, wood, wire etc. Of these perhaps clay is the easiest material to use. To make a stamp, roll out a short thick coil of clay, leaving enough of a stem to allow the stamp to be held comfortably when in use. Make several at the same time. Flatten one end by pressing on a smooth, flat surface, until the head is of the required diameter, bearing in mind that the stamps will shrink. Leave to dry until almost leatherhard before cutting or carving your design into the flat face of the stamp. Alternatively, you can cut away, leaving the design in relief. When the stamps are completely dry, fire to a biscuit temperature. If fired to a high

Anglo-Saxon pot, England, 5th-9th centuries AD, 24 cm/dia. Decorated with two different designs of stamps and incised lines. *Ashmolean Museum Oxford (1927.77).*

Jug by Sheila Casson (UK), 1993, 12.5 cm/h. Impressed decoration. The 'flower' shape stamp was made from a piece of wire, twisted into shape. Salt-glazed. *Photograph by Ben Casson.*

temperature, the stamps become non-porous and will stick if used on soft, slightly wet clay.

Several effects can be achieved when using stamps. A decorative pattern can be built up by repeatedly pressing in a single stamp, or by using a combination of stamps of different designs. When using stamps an effect similar to that of applying sprigs can be achieved by rubbing a small piece of very soft clay onto the surface of the pot before pressing in a stamp. This has the effect of creating a raised surface pattern. The photograph of a jug by Sheila Casson (UK) shows the use of a stamp, which was made from a piece of wire, and illustrates yet another variation of the decorative effects it is possible to achieve using stamps. Many ceramicists use stamps to mark their work for identification purposes. Fired clay stamps are probably the most widely used type, but carved soapstone stamps,

commercially-made rubber or metal stamps, or stamps made from wood or plaster are also used.

Current practices

For many potters, the use of stamps is an important element in the decoration of their work. Among them is Maureen Minchin (UK) who uses a variety of decorating techniques, including stamps,

Right
Box with lid by Maureen Minchin (UK). Slab-built, stamped and sprigged decoration. Raku-fired.

Below
Jars with lids by John Glick (USA), 1985, largest 25 cm/dia. Incised and stamped decoration (using bisqued porcelain stamps) under multiple glazes. Porcelain. *Photograph by Dirk Bakker.*

in creating the slabs from which she constructs her raku-fired caskets. Bisque-fired stamps, sprigs made in biscuit-fired moulds, pieces of wood and found objects such as nuts and bolts, are used to build up richly textured surfaces, which are further enhanced by the raku firing. Having cut out slabs to the required shapes, Maureen begins the pattern by pressing a large bisque-fired stamp into the centre of each slab. Then, using the end of a length of wood, two rows of triangular shaped impressions are made, to create a border around the edges of the slabs. Pellets of clay are applied in the V-shaped areas of the border, and small leaf-shaped stamps are pressed into them. Next leaf-shaped sprigs are applied. These are made in a biscuit-fired mould, which was made by repeatedly pressing a biscuit-fired stamp into a slab of clay. In this way several sprigs can be made at one time. Once this stage of the decoration has been completed, the body

of the casket is assembled while the clay is still relatively soft. Coils of clay are added inside to reinforce the joints. Next the feet are added. These are made from narrow slabs of clay which are rolled up into cylindrical shapes. The modelled hare and support (which is made in the same way as the feet of the casket) are added to the lid, which is then put in place over the gable ends of the base. Pieces of clay are added at the corners of the base and on the apex of the lid, which are then stamped. After the biscuit firing a copper wash is sometimes applied and cleaned off, so that colour remains only in the crevices. Underglaze colours and glazes are applied before the piece is raku fired. Maureen says of her work,

> Most of the techniques I use arise from my original interest in salt glaze, where impressing and sprigging are commonly used. I like the 'formality' of these techniques. The decoration has many influences, historic and current – Saxon and Medieval pottery and German Salt glaze, to name a few.

Decorated slabs ready for assembling.

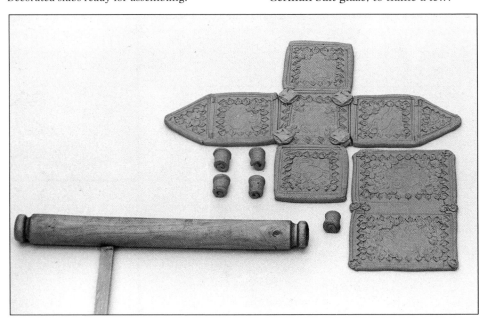

Much of the feeling of spontaneity in these pieces is achieved by decorating and assembling while the clay is still in a fairly soft state. The clay retains an appearance of softness after firing.

A single stamp can be impressed several times to build up a complex pattern. This is one of the techniques used by Scott Frankenberger, an American potter working in Indiana. Scott uses stamps made from a variety of materials, including bisque-fired clay, carved wood – lengths of dowel with designs carved on both ends – and heat cut styrofoam (see photograph below). With a background in drawing and printmaking, Scott cites experience in these disciplines as a contributing factor to his use of impressed decoration in his work, combined with a period spent in Indonesia, where the use of block printmaking and pattern build-up in batik fabrics is widely practised. In Scott's work

The completed box prior to firing. *Photographs by Sean Leahy.*

Stamps made from styrofoam, Scott Frankenberger.

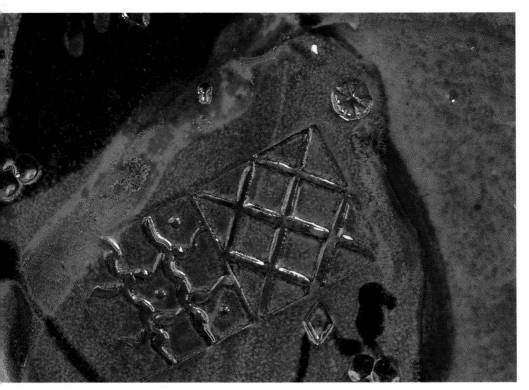

Detail of tray 25 × 20 × 2.5 cm by Scott Frankenberger (USA), 1994. Impressed pattern made with styrofoam blocks. Porcelain.

large areas of complex patterns are created by repeating single units. By using this and other decorating techniques, Scott aims to 'create an active clay surface'. He works in porcelain, making a wide range of mostly functional pottery, including serving trays, covered jars and baking dishes. A number of different glazes are used, which overlap and give a sense of depth to the richly textured surfaces of Scott's work.

Most potters who use stamps seem to use them in combination with other decorating techniques. In addition to those already mentioned, Jane Hamlyn, Svend Bayer, Takeshi Yasuda and Lara Scobie, all of whose work is described in other chapters, use stamps. The work of these potters clearly illustrates the versatility of impressed stamps as a method of decoration.

Chapter Four
Roulettes

A roulette or roller stamp is a cylinder which has a design in relief on its edge so that when rolled on soft clay, a continuous impressed pattern is created.

History

The technique of rolling a textured object of a basically cylindrical shape across an area of soft clay is known to have been used by potters early on in the Jomon period in Japan. The earliest of the widespread patterns to be used was zig-zag rouletting. This was followed by elliptical rouletting – three elliptical depressions were carved in a band around a small stick; beneath these another three filled the intervals, and so on until about six bands of ellipses were completed. When rolled on soft clay this carved stick created a continuous pattern of small irregular oval shapes in relief on the surface. Rolling parallel to the rim was the commonest method of using the roulette and sometimes rouletting was continued inside the pot and on top of the rim. Other designs used included diamond and fishnet patterns.

Decorating clay surfaces with a roulette was used on pottery produced in Europe (*c.* 500 – 50 BC). It was known as La Téne pottery. It has a distinctive curvilinear decoration. Roulette wheels, probably not unlike the pastry wheels of today, were

Jar, Greenware, China. 3rd-4th centuries AD, 9 cm/h. Roulette and stamp patterns. *Ashmolean Museum Oxford (1956.3925).*

used to make small, square-notched marks on the surface of pots. Arched lines created by these roulettes were combined with other methods of decoration such as stamps and incising. Patterns in which roulettes were used include diamond-shaped outlines bordering stamps, usually circular in shape; chevrons and crosshatching.

In China for a period during the Southern dynasties (Six Dynasties) (AD 265–589), wheel-thrown pots, glazed in an iron glaze were made which had decoration comprising of rouletting and stamping. Wide shouldered jars – some with lids and attached lugs, bowls and basins, have bands of rouletted decoration made up of rows of diamond-shaped impressions, bordered by two bands of stamped impressions (see photograph on page 35). On some pots the rouletting is seen to overlap, while on others the join is concealed behind an applied sprig, in the shape of an animal mask, for example.

Rouletting was used as a decorating technique on English Medieval pottery. It is to be found particularly on cooking pots, bowls and pitchers from the earlier periods, when roulettes were often used to decorate applied strips of clay. Examples of rouletting can be found on some 13th century jugs from Yorkshire. These were squat in form, yellow glazed and decorated with complex rouletted patterns.

Traditional potters in many parts of Africa use various methods of creating rouletted patterns. Materials used include carved wood, plaited grasses and dried corn husks. Some of the roulettes made from grass are intricately interwoven and create varied and interesting patterns when rolled on a clay surface. The rouletted patterns are often combined with other types of decoration such as incising and painting with slip.

Technique

It is possible to make roulettes from several different materials. Of these clay is perhaps the easiest to use, wood and plaster being other possible materials. When making roulettes, a number of considerations are important. First of all, decide whether you want to make a narrow or fairly broad band of decoration. A narrow band can be repeated or used in combination with other roulette patterns. Next to be considered is the design itself. Designs for roulettes are often of a type which it is possible to join up almost seamlessly round the circumference of a pot.

To make a clay roulette, first make a cylinder of the required size, using fine grained, ungrogged clay. It should then be left to dry to the leatherhard stage before making a hole (for the axle) through the centre, using a teapot spout hole maker or some such implement. Remember to allow for shrinkage, as the axle must turn freely within the hole of the fired roulette. Next carve the design. Once the cylinder has dried to bone dry, the carving can be refined/tidied up, before it is fired to biscuit temperature.

The easiest handle/axle to use is a single piece of strong wire (coat hanger wire for example) which is passed through the hole, until the roulette is in the middle of the length of wire. Then bend the wire up at both sides (allowing enough space for the roulette to turn freely) and twist the ends together to form a handle. More elaborate and comfortable handles can be made from wood, or by using ready-made handles from old handtools. When using a roulette to decorate a pot, the clay should be supported with one hand on the inside, as pressure is applied with the roulette on the outside.

Rouletting as a technique offers the potter an infinite variety of patterns. However, having made several, you will probably find yourself using the same few, time and again, as it is not until you have used them that you will be able to decide whether the pattern created is to your liking or not, or whether the texture it makes is appropriate decoration for the kind of work you make.

Current practices

Jonathan Garratt is a wood-fire potter who makes extensive use of rouletted decoration in his work. The following is

The roulette is rolled on the surface as the pot is supported on the inside.

A selection of the roulettes and cord rollers used by Jonathan Garratt.

an account of the technique he uses. Having thrown a pot, throwing rings are smoothed and slurry is removed, using a throwing rib. If the slurry is not removed, the roulette will stick. Next the surface is

The completed pattern.

the decoration. If you bevel the roulette to the extent that only the central third of the potential impression is used you get a more uniform and flowing pattern. Having made the basic clay shape, Jonathan rolls it into a textured surface to impart a pattern on to the edge of the roulette. Surfaces used include textured shoe soles, corduroy fabric, basket weave, Surform blade, rubber mats etc. On applying textured patterns to roulettes, Jonathan comments,

it can be a bit hit and miss – usually miss! On the other hand, I find that too correct an impression gives pots a mechanical feel which I find unsympathetic. If the impression on the roulette is a bit wonky, the resulting pattern often has a greater depth of interest.

Included in Jonathan's collection of roulettes are some made from found objects – beads from jewellery shops, a plastic wheel from a toy tractor, a length of splined dowel from a hardware shop. He also has a selection of wooden roulettes made by carving/cutting patterns in short lengths of broom handle or narrow dowel. Some of the influences in Jonathan's work are Chinese and European Neolithic pottery, West African textiles, Zulu shields and Medieval French Rouen jugs.

Other contemporary potters who make use of rouletting in their work include Jane Hamlyn, Phil Rogers and Lara Scobie. These three potters use found mechanical parts, cogs and cog wheels, as roulettes to create very different effects. Jane Hamlyn uses a cog from a child's toy to create narrow, notched lines, often running diagonally from the base of a pot to the rim. These indented lines are further accentuated as a result of being salt glazed. (See Chapter 10; including the

lightly washed with water, using a soft brush (Japanese/Chinese type) – this prevents the roller from sticking to the clay surface. Roulettes made from clay need to be soaked before use. Starting at the top of the pot (which is still on the wheel), the roulette is rolled on the surface around the pot. Jonathan prefers to leave part of the surface at the bottom of some pots undecorated, as he considers that this gives the pot a certain lift. Total rouletting can be a bit deadening he feels. In his opinion rouletting 'imbues the pots with a certain quality that makes for interest but is not loud. Combined with the irregularities of wood-firing, even a uniform pattern can provide something of a canvas for the flames to decorate.'

Jonathan uses all kinds of materials and found objects to make roulettes. For roulettes to be used to create large areas of texture, as opposed to single bands of decoration, he first of all makes a sausage of clay which is as even as possible, and bevelled a little towards the ends. The reason for bevelling the roulette is to avoid lines between the bands of the pattern, which tend to give a static feel to

Lidded pot by Jonathan Garratt (UK), 19 cm/h × 17.5 cm/dia. Rouletted pattern. Wood-fired earthenware. *Photograph by Paul Adair.*

photograph on page 68.) Phil Rogers uses a cylindrical roller (from the internal workings of a rotary pencil sharpener) to create all over 'lined' texture on the surface of some of his pots. (See Chapter 5.) Lara Scobie also uses a cylindrical roller, which is one of the many objects she uses to create a wide range of textures on her porcelain vessels. (See Chapter 9.)

In common with many of the other decorating techniques in this book, rouletting can be used as part of an overall scheme for decorating by combining it with other techniques. For instance, a line made with a very narrow roulette can act as a frame for other decoration. Rouletting can also be the initial stage in creating inlaid patterns.

39

Chapter Five
Paddles

The technique of using textured wooden paddles to impart a pattern on pots more than likely developed from the use of lengths of wood or plain paddles in the construction of hand-built pots, where they would have been used both to compress and join coils of clay, and also to beat the pots into more regular shapes. An anvil – a smooth rounded stone or a similar fired clay or wooden shape – was used to support the pot on the inside, while it was being beaten on the outside.

History

The use of the paddle and anvil technique was widespread throughout prehistoric South East Asia. Pots formed in this way which have been found at Ban Chiang in North East Thailand are up to 4,000 years old. Traditional potters in Thailand today in an area near Ban Chiang use the paddle and the anvil technique in the making of water jars and cooking pots. The shoulders of these pots are sometimes decorated with a stamped geometric design made with a carved wooden paddle.

During the Shang Dynasty in China (c.1600 – 1027 BC), round bottomed vessels were made by beating the clay on the outside with a paddle which had a crisscrossed pattern against a stone held on the inside. In other instances pots have patterns which may have been created by beating with textile-covered paddles. The rims of these hand-built pots were then shaped and trued on a wheel.

In an area of the Madang Province of Papua New Guinea, where pots are formed by the paddle and anvil (rounded stone) technique, carved wooden paddles are used to create raised patterns, made up of a combination of roughly square and round marks. In addition to Thailand and Papua New Guinea, variations on the paddle and anvil technique are used by traditional potters in many other countries including Nigeria, Namibia, Sudan, India, the Philippines, Korea and Japan.

Technique

Using a carved wooden paddle to impress a pattern on the surface of a pot can either be carried out on wet pots still on the wheel, or when the pot is soft leatherhard. Working at this latter stage, one option is to use a plain paddle or length of wood to alter the pot's shape by beating it, to square it off, or to create a number of facets around the circumference. Then using a textured paddle, a pattern can be impressed into each facet. If bulbous shapes are beaten with a paddle, only a section of it will come into contact with the surface, resulting in circular areas of impressed patterns. Another option is to repeatedly apply the paddle, creating an all over pattern comprised of overlapping areas of texture. When using a plain length of wood, for instance to create facets on a thrown pot, if the wood has a pronounced grain, then a pattern will be imparted onto the flattened facets. This can create an interesting effect, which becomes more pronounced after a glaze firing, as the glaze tends to break on the higher edges, and pool in the grooves made by the wood grain. Wooden bats with parallel grooved lines, used in the past for forming butter into regular shapes, make ideal paddles for decorating pots.

The easiest way to make a paddle is to get a length of wood approximately 30 × 9 × 2 cm in size. Various patterns can then be cut or carved into the surface. Simple patterns comprised of parallel lines or a crosshatch pattern, can easily be cut with a handsaw, while more complex patterns will need to be carried out using wood-carving tools. Another variation on the use of paddles is to wrap cord horizontally around a piece of wood and use this to create texture on the surface of pots. It is best to use hardwood if possible to make paddles, especially if you are going to be using them often, as softwood is not as durable when wetted

frequently. Hardwood has another advantage in that it is easier to create a distinct impression when using a heavier piece of wood. When making paddles it is a good idea to cut/carve a different pattern on each side. If you want to make a wide paddle, it will be easier to use if you cut out a handle shape at the top of the piece of wood.

Current practices

Phil Rogers (UK) uses a variety of textured wooden paddles to decorate his pots, including a cord wrapped length of wood, a butter paddle, and a paddle with a cut pattern. The technique he uses is as follows. Having thrown a cylinder with a

A selection of the tools used by Phil Rogers to create textured surfaces, including three paddles: a cord wrapped length of wood, a butter paddle and a length of wood with a cut, cross-hatch pattern.

Beating a freshly thrown pot with a textured paddle.

Throwing of the pot is completed after the surface has been paddled. *Photographs by Richard Davies, USA.*

fairly thick base, and with the top opening large enough to allow him to get his hand inside to support the wall, the outside is beaten with a wet wooden paddle so that the pattern is imprinted in relief onto the surface. As the pattern is applied all the way around the pot, the 'strikes' must be done rhythmically, firmly and with confidence, otherwise the imprint may be indistinct or misplaced. Once the pattern has been completed, Phil continues to shape the pot from the inside, by pushing his fingers gently outwards as the wheel rotates. This expanding of the shape, also expands the pattern. Phil considers that this latter

process harmonises the pattern with the form. He points out that paddling can be carried out at the soft leatherhard stage instead, with certain shapes or with partially thrown pots, which will have a neck added to them later. When decorating with a textured wooden paddle at the leatherhard stage, the paddle must be dry or it will stick to the surface.

Many potters and clay artists continue to experiment with surface textures and qualities throughout their careers. It is as though the satisfying feeling resulting from manipulating clay that is experienced when we first come in

Jar by Phil Rogers (UK), 30.5 cm/h. Paddled texture. The wall of the pot has been pushed out to form facets. Salt-glazed stoneware.

contact with the material, continues to excite and encourages us to try out more techniques, to alter and enrich the clay surface. Warren MacKenzie has at different times fluted, faceted and paddled the surfaces of his pots or altered them by any one of several other methods, to create a wide range of shapes and textures. When using a patterned wooden butter paddle to create a textured surface, the decoration is carried out on freshly thrown pots, while they are still on the wheel head. Speaking about his approach to decoration during an interview published in *The Studio Potter* (vol. 19, no. 1, Dec. 1990), Warren said that he relies on a 'richness of surface form' in his work and he continued, 'I try therefore to use glazes that reveal form by changing colour where they run thick or thin, or by being transparent to reveal what is taking place on the clay surface beneath'.

Australian potter Janet Mansfield, known for her salt-glazed and wood-fired work, sometimes uses textured wooden paddles to decorate her pots. Writing of her work in her book, *Salt-glaze Ceramics An International Perspective*, Janet describes her making process and explains that she particularly likes to make large jars in three or more pieces and assemble them while still soft. When a piece is leatherhard, she often uses a carved wooden paddle to create texture. While beating the outside of the pot, a ball of soft clay wrapped in plastic is held against the inside, both to offer resistance to the beating and to retain the shape of the pot. Surface texture created by this type of decoration is highlighted and accentuated by the salt-glaze process. Sometimes a slip or a pour of ash glaze is applied to create a contrast with the salt-glazed surface.

As with many of the techniques described in other chapters, applying texture by using a carved wooden paddle can be regarded as a starting point rather than a complete decorative technique in itself. As can be seen from the sequence of photographs showing Phil Rogers at work, the shaping of a pot can continue once the surface has been textured with a paddle, enlarging/altering/softening the pattern. Alternatively, other decorative techniques can be used in combination with paddled decoration.

Jar with lid by Warren MacKenzie (USA). Impressed pattern created by beating with a textured wooden butter paddle.

Chapter Six
Impressing Large Areas

This chapter is concerned with techniques whereby large areas of texture are impressed at one go, as opposed to creating a large pattern by repeating a single impression, as is the case when using rolled cord, roulettes, paddles etc.

History

Mat impressions creating large areas of texture are to be found on the bases of many prehistoric pots from different countries and periods. It is considered that these impressions result from the pots having been hand-built on sections of matting, which allowed them to be rotated as the potter worked on them. These marks are often so sharply imprinted that it seems clear that they could not have been made by accident. It is likely that prior to starting to build up the walls of pots, some potters began by pressing the base firmly down on the mat they used.

On some Neolithic Chinese pottery, dating from the 5th to the 4th millennium BC, the bases show impressions of basketwork apparently made of bamboo strips. Other bases have impressions of a coarse woven fabric made of hemp or similar fibres. Again the pots would have been placed on these surfaces to allow for turning as they were

being made. Pots with woven mat impressions on the bases have also been found on the Cycladic Islands. These conical cups were made by the Keros-Syros culture and date from c.2,700 – 2,200 BC (see also leaf impressions in Chapter 1).

Examples of areas of impressed texture larger than the base of pots are to be seen on some pots made during the Meroitic Period (c.300BC–AD400) in Nubia (the ancient land of Nubia, part of the Nile Valley, is today divided between Egypt and the Republic of the Sudan). Large round-bottomed storage jars have impressions of matting or coarse fabric covering the exterior surface with only

Large jar with bottle neck, Meroe, Nubia, approx. 74 cm/h × 50 cm/dia. The body has an all over texture. The neck is undecorated.
© *The Trustees of the National Museums of Scotland 1996 (1910.110.6).*

the neck areas remaining untextured (see photograph on the previous page).

Today in some areas of Nigeria, as a result of the technique used to form round bottomed pots (a variation of the paddle and anvil technique), large areas of texture are created on the body of the pot. A coarse-textured cloth covers a shallow, concave mould shape. The pot is formed on this by beating from the inside. The texture from the fabric is imprinted onto the body of the pot while the coiled neck (added later) is left plain.

Technique

By far the easiest method of impressing large areas of texture into clay at one go is to use a rolling pin or for bigger areas, a slab roller. Using these methods a wide variety of natural and manmade textures can be pressed into slabs of clay, these slabs then being used as required. When using a slab roller, having rolled a slab of the appropriate size and thickness, arrange the textured object(s) on it. Then cover with the backing cloth and pass under the roller again. If the object being used is fairly thick, you will need to adjust the measurement between the roller and the base accordingly. Otherwise the object may become so deeply embedded in the clay, that it will be difficult to remove it without distorting the impression or damaging the slab. A certain amount of trial and error will be involved in finding the appropriate consistency of clay to use for particular textures. If the slabs of clay are too hard, then it will be difficult to produce an impression which has sufficient definition.

Porcelain slip is brushed onto slabs over an open weave fabric.

Current practices

Jim Robison (USA/UK) uses textured slabs in the creation of his large-scale ceramic sculptures. Slabs are rolled out initially on a slab roller, which he made from an antique washing mangle. One of the techniques which Jim employs involves the use of various fabrics which have a loose open weave. Strips of these fabrics are arranged on slabs of clay and are rolled well into them. Porcelain slip is then brushed onto the fabric which acts as a stencil, so that a slip pattern remains when the fabric is removed. This results in two different effects – the net-like impression where the fabric was embedded in the clay and the stencilled slip pattern. Different decorative techniques are used on other areas of the slabs. For example, having applied a coating of slip, it is then combed with a

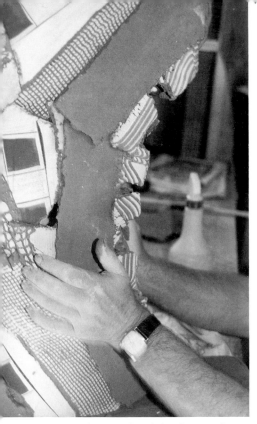

Fragments of textured and slip-decorated slabs are assembled to form a standing sculptural vase form. *Photographs by Sue Crossland.*

Sculptural Vase Form by Jim Robison (USA/UK), 1 metre/h. Some of the textures on this piece were created by impressing pieces of open weave cloth into the clay slabs. *Photograph by Nick Broomhead.*

comb made from a rubber kidney. In addition to the decorated slabs, plain slabs which have torn irregular edges are also used. Slab fragments are arranged over two wooden formers which have been covered with newspapers to prevent the clay from sticking. The two sections will later be joined to form a standing sculptural vase form. Once the two main sections have stiffened sufficiently to allow them to stand, additional slab fragments are sometimes added. Layers of ash glazes are sprayed on the pieces.

Jim's inspiration for the forms and textures of these pieces comes from elements of the landscape – rock formations and megaliths – found in the area of West Yorkshire where he lives. The tones of the ash glazes on the fired

Embossed wallpaper is rolled into clay slab to create a relief pattern. *Photograph from Jane Hamlyn.*

Quatrefoil Dish by Jane Hamlyn (UK). Interior pattern created by rolling textured wallpaper on the slab from which the base was formed. *Photograph by Haru Sameshima.*

Jar, China, Late Zhou Dynasty, 4th-3rd centuries BC, approx. 12 cm/h. Impressed pattern. Earthenware. *Ashmolean Museum, Oxford (1956.1877).*

sculptures also reflect and echo the colours of the surrounding landscape.

Salt-glaze potter Jane Hamlyn makes extensive use of embossed wallpapers and a slab roller to make the bases for her range of very distinctive dishes. In making these pots a ring of clay is thrown, distorted, then joined to the slab rolled, textured base (see photograph on page 47). These areas of textured patterns respond well to being salt glazed and are further enriched and enlivened as a result.

Large areas of impressed texture are perhaps best suited as components of work, bases of dishes, sections of large sculptures etc. As with many of the other techniques discussed so far, this is a method of creating texture which can be successfully combined with other techniques.

Chapter Seven
Handles/Feet

This chapter deals with using impressed marks in the making and decorating of handles and feet to be attached to pots.

History

On many prehistoric and historic pots, the method of decoration used on the body was also used to decorate the handle(s). This is a feature of some handled Beakers from the late Neolithic and Early Bronze Age. Comb teeth impressions, fingernail impressions or incising used on the body are also present on the handle. Decorated handles are also to be found on food vessels of these periods. On a two-handled food vessel from Kinross in Perthshire, Scotland (see photograph below), the body is decorated with whipped cord impressions (marks made by impressing a twisted cord that has been wrapped round itself or another material, thus giving short, segmented impressions). Under the rim there are two lines made by impressing a twisted cord. The lower line extends down onto the lug handles and along their centres before continuing in a line around the pot, just above the base. These lines act as borders to the areas of whipped cord impressions, as well as linking the handles visually to the body of the pot.

Food Vessel, Kinross, Scotland, *c.*1900–1700 BC, 4.4 cm/h 9.6 cm/dia. Twisted cord and whipped cord impressions. © *The Trustees of the National Museums of Scotland 1996 (EQ 795).*

Current practices

For many potters, the most direct method of decorating a handle is to create incised lines or ridges during the process of pulling a handle. However this is just one approach. Others have come up with inventive and imaginative means of decorating and applying textures to the coiled handles and feet they make, so that they are in keeping with the pots to which they are attached. Not just appendages or afterthoughts, but features which accentuate the overall forms, so that a unifying whole is created. One potter whose work comes to mind immediately in this context is Takeshi Yasuda (Japan/UK).

I have seen Takeshi demonstrate his techniques for making handles and feet on several occasions. What struck me most was not the surfaces on which he rolled out the coils of clay, or even the resulting textures, but the manner in which he then dexterously manipulated the coils, to transform them into wonderfully fluid shapes, which, while attractive in themselves, completely transformed the thrown pots to which they were attached.

The technique Takeshi uses is as follows. Coils of clay are made using a coil-making tool, invented and made by Takeshi ('Takeshi Yasuda's Amazing Portion Controller Coil Machine'). This tool consists of a rectangular-shaped board with a hole in each corner. A bolt, a nut, two washers and a wing nut are placed in each hole. The height the board is raised off the work surface, and thus the thickness of the coil is altered by adjusting the positions of the nuts on the bolts accordingly. To make a coil, a roughly shaped sausage of clay is placed on a smooth surface. The board is placed on top, resting on the ends of the four

bolts. It is then pushed forwards and pulled backwards and in this way, regular shaped coils are produced. Prior to rolling the coils on a textured surface, each one is rolled on a thin coating of cornflour, sprinkled from a small muslin bag. This prevents the coil of clay from sticking to the textured surface. A flat piece of wood is used to apply even pressure, as the coil is rolled slowly on the texture. The surfaces which Takeshi uses include a section from the cover of a fluorescent light – a piece of plastic with parallel grooves – and a piece of wire mesh from a meat safe.

Once the coil has been textured, it is slapped down onto an even surface to flatten the back, creating a strap-like cross section. The coil is trimmed, the ends are folded in, and it is further manipulated into the required shape. The areas on the pot where the handles will be attached are roughened with the prongs of a fork and a coating of slip is applied with a brush. Handles made in this way are attached to Takeshi's 'Sprung Bottom Bowls', 'Large Platters' and 'Pillow Dishes' (see page 55). The feet attached to his 'Plateau on Three Feet' are made in the same way.

Other techniques used by Takeshi to texture handles involves the use of a ruler. For one type of handle, a ruler edge is impressed diagonally into a coil of clay as it is being rolled, resulting in a deeply indented spiral. This style of handle is generally attached as an arched shape to

Right, above
A regularly shaped coil is produced using 'Takeshi Yasuda's Amazing Portion Controller Coil Machine'.

Right, below
A coil is rolled on a textured surface, in this instance a section of wire from a meat safe.

Takeshi's 'Bucket' forms, or as a side handle to teapots. For another type of handle, a coil is made as described above, then formed into a soft triangular shape, by slapping down first one side, then another, and then the base, onto a flat surface. A ruler edge is pressed in lengthwise to the coil, to make two parallel grooved lines. The base of the coil is then slapped down on the flat surface again, to soften the impressed lines. This type of handle is attached to teapots in an arched shape.

A white slip is applied when pots are soft leatherhard. They are then biscuit fired. After glazing in the base glaze, thick

Left, above
Manipulating a textured coil to form a handle.

Left, below
The completed handle is attached to a thrown dish. *Photographs by Paul Adair.*

splotches of green and brown glazes (the base glaze with additions of copper and manganese respectively) are applied. During the glaze firing the coloured glazes run and flow, creating an effect which is reminiscent of the 'Nara Sansai Ware', made in the 8th century in Japan.

Another variation on the rolled handle theme is used by American potter Scott Frankenberger. A section of linoleum, as used for lino printing, is glued onto a wooden backing such as chipboard. Then, using lino cutting tools, a pattern is cut into the lino, perhaps a series of linear grooves or a more complex design (see photograph below). A coil of clay is then rolled on the lino, resulting in a textured surface. Handles made in this way are attached to baking dishes, casseroles etc. Carved slabs of clay which

Carved lino blocks for making textured, coiled handles (Scott Frankenberger).

Dish by Jane Hamlyn (UK). The pattern on the handles and feet was created by rolling on a rubber car mat. *Photograph by Bill Thomas.*

have been biscuit fired can be used as an alternative to lino, to create a textured surface for handle rolling.

Jane Hamlyn creates her richly textured handles by rolling coils of clay on a variety of rubber car mats, each with a different texture/pattern. She also uses a surface made up from strips of decorative wooden mouldings. These handles are used as side handles on Jane's mugs and

jugs, as lug handles on large covered dishes and as handles on lids. To make other types of handles Jane uses a ruler edge, rolled diagonally along a coil of clay to make a shallow impressed spiral line. All of the textures created by these techniques show up particularly well after salt glazing.

The possibilities for decorating coiled handles by impressing are endless. Other techniques include flattening a coil into a strap shape by rolling a roulette along it lengthwise, or flattening the coil into an

Sprung Bottom Bowl by Takeshi Yasuda (Japan/UK), 34 × 32 × 16 cm. The pattern on the handles was created by rolling on a textured surface. Oxidised stoneware.

oval strap shape, by pressing down on it with a flat piece of wood, prior to applying the roulette. Alternatively, rolled cord decoration could be used at this stage. Another possibility is to press all or part of the surface of a stamp repeatedly into a coiled handle after it has been attached to a pot. This method is also suitable for decorating coiled handles on lids.

Chapter Eight
Altering Forms by Impressing

All of the prehistoric, historic and contemporary pots which have been discussed so far, as displaying examples of impressed decoration, have generally been impressed on the surface only, so that the shapes of the pots themselves were not altered or distorted in any way. Natural, manmade objects or stamps pressed into the surface, but not with enough pressure as to distort the pot; roulettes or cord rolled on, again just affecting the surface. The exception is perhaps decorating with a carved wooden paddle. In order to imprint a distinct pattern, a paddle must be beaten firmly against the wall of a pot, an action which invariably creates facets, especially on a rounded form.

This chapter is about making impressed marks which go beyond surface decoration. Impressions which are so deep or made so forcefully, that the form of the original pot or pot section is permanently altered.

Technique

Perhaps the easiest and most satisfying stage at which to alter the shape of a pot using impressed marks is just after it has been thrown, pressing in either with a finger, the edge of a throwing rib, a piece of wood etc. If pressure is applied with the edge of a throwing rib, while the wheel is slowly turning, a series of indented diagonal lines will be created. By impressing vertical lines, again using the straight edge of a throwing rib or a ruler edge, a pot can be divided into a number

of lobes. It is important to remember to support the wall of the pot with one hand on the inside, while pressing in a rib on the outside, to achieve a definite, dented, linear effect.

The shape of a pot can also be altered by impressing at the leatherhard stage, using a number of different methods: beating with a textured paddle, not only to create a surface pattern, but also to facet the pot; or a technique similar to pressing in a throwing rib at the soft stage, but which creates a very different, crisper effect, is to beat the soft leatherhard pot, with the edge of a wooden or metal implement.

Current practices

The following are examples of different methods used by four potters to alter the form of their pots. Some of the techniques described are suitable for use on freshly thrown pots; others for pots which have dried to leatherhard. Wood-fire potter Robert Sanderson (UK) writes as follows about one of the methods he uses to alter the form of 'firm leatherhard' pots.

This particular style of impressed/ beaten decoration developed by way of lateral thinking. All my work is hand-thrown and wood-fired. I am particularly attracted to the wood-fire effect on an unglazed surface. Because the flame is in contact with the pots during the firing, the patterns left on the clay surface tend to reflect the passage of that flame. By deliberately

juxtaposing pots, stacking them on top of one another, or leaning them against one another, I am able to take advantage of the fired colours created by the shadows cast onto neighbouring pots. Where the form is altered and then stacked very close to (almost touching) another pot, the impression formed in the clay surface is accentuated by the flame markings. The overall effect is a combination of

Using the edge of a length of wood vertical lines are impressed, dividing the pot into a number of lobes.

both deliberate/conscious deforming of the clay, and the unpredictable scorch marks (flashing and fly-ash) of the flame during the firing. The altering of the pot can be minimal, however the fired result can be very effective.

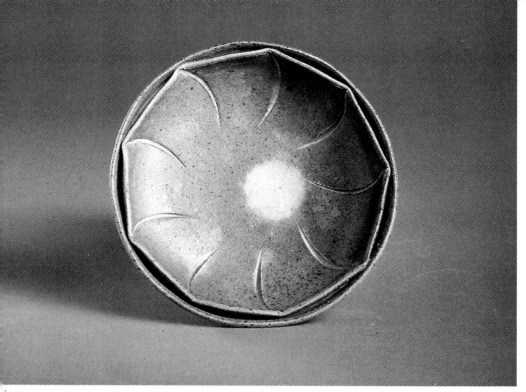

Bowl by Warren MacKenzie (USA). After throwing, the two parts of the split rim were pressed together using a throwing rib. This action also created the impressed lines on the interior. Salt-glazed.

A small teapot with beaten impressed lines on two sides. *Photographs by Paul Adair.*

Teapot by Robert Sanderson (UK), 1994,
9 cm/h. Thrown and altered, beaten with
wooden edge. Wood-fired stoneware.
Photograph by Paul Adair.

This style of beaten decoration can be carried out at various stages of 'leatherhardness'. However, the softer the clay, the greater the impression created and the larger the area of that impression; the harder the clay, the smaller the area of the impression. Having divided the pot into as many equal segments as required (in this case four), by marking the shoulder of the pot with a swipe of a wet finger, the impressions are first made on the two sides opposite to one another. Then the remaining impressions are made on the other two sides. This method of working from opposite sides, helps to equalise any deformation of the pot. The final impression also causes the rim of the pot to return to the 'round'.

Warren MacKenzie uses many different techniques to alter his thrown pots. Many of these involve making impressions of one kind or another, on freshly thrown pots. One example of this is as follows. A shallow dish is thrown with a double or split rim. The two edges of the rim are joined at regular intervals, by pressing them together from the inside, using a throwing rib. This action alters the shape of the dish, as well as producing an impressed pattern on the interior (see photograph on page 58). Another technique involves the use of a small round plastic lid from a container. When a shallow bowl has been thrown, the ring of the container cover is held in position against the wall on the outside and pressed slightly into the surface. At the same time, pressure is applied from inside the bowl, slightly pushing the clay into

Articulated Jug by Walter Keeler (UK). The impressed line on the top section was created by hitting with the edge of a metal file before it was joined to the lower section. Salt-glazed.

the hollow form and creating a regular circular mound on the exterior of the pot. This action is repeated a number of times, working around the pot, to complete the decoration.

Salt-glaze potter Walter Keeler (UK) uses impressed marks both to add definition to and alter the shape of some of his thrown and constructed pots. With two deft slaps of the edge of a metal file, he can transform thrown shapes – a teapot spout or the upper section of an articulated jug (see photographs). A thrown teapot body is eased into an oval shape and attached to a base, before being hit with the file edge to create two distinct vertical lines, one at each side. These crisp impressed/beaten lines immediately attract our attention in the finished pieces, as they are further accentuated as a result of the salt-glaze process. The line created by the file is sometimes complemented by a carefully placed stamp, which leaves a double concentric circle impression.

Teapot (detail showing spout) by Walter Keeler. A thrown spout was altered by beating with the edge of a metal file.

The form of a pot can be subtly altered when using stamps, if the clay surface is still fairly soft. This is a technique used by Takeshi Yasuda, particularly on teapots and tall jugs. Prior to pressing in the stamp, pellets of clay are put on the surface of the pot while it is still quite soft. The pressure of applying the stamp creates a gentle dent, which slightly distorts the form. These dents are further accentuated by the pooling of the runny green and brown glazes which Takeshi uses on his work. The combination of the dents and glaze quality has the effect of visually softening the overall forms.

The work of these four potters clearly illustrates that making impressed marks which alter the form of a pot, either subtly or very definitely, is a technique which offers many creative possibilities.

Chapter Nine
Entire forms

This chapter is concerned with forms which have impressed textures covering all, or nearly all, of their exterior surfaces.

History

Few vessels of the Japanese Jomon Period are without any ornamentation whatever. Most have decoration over a large part of the surface and many are completely covered in decoration. Particularly during the Middle Jomon period some extremely ornate pots were produced. These pots are unlike others of the Jomon period in that they do not rely solely on surface decoration of the body for their ornamentation. Typical of these pieces are large, richly adorned, often fantastic forms with perforated rims, which have exotic decoration. While cord marking is still evident on some pieces (see chapter on Cord), it is usually combined with other types of decoration e.g. incised marks, stick marking, perforations, applied and indented ridges, combing etc.

As already described in the chapters on Impressions made with Manmade Objects and with Cord (Chapters 1 and 2), two popular types of decoration on Beakers of the Neolithic and Early Bronze Age are 'All Over Cord' (see photograph on page 23) and 'All Over Comb'. In both instances, the twisted cord and the comb were often used to make impressed, encircling lines, repeated around the pot,

Left
Food vessels, Stirlingshire (Rt.), *c.*2000–1900 BC and Argyll (Lt.), *c.*2150 BC Scotland, 14.5 cm/h and 9.7 cm/h. On the pot on the right the whole exterior surface is decorated with rows of triangular impressions. The pot on the left has lines of comb teeth impressions and triangular impressions. © *The Trustees of the National Museums of Scotland 1996 (EE 167, Rt., HPO 11, Lt.).*

until the whole of the exterior surface was covered.

These are just two examples of prehistoric pottery types which have all over decoration. In the chapters on different forms of incised pottery, further examples will be described.

Current practices

Lara Scobie constructs sculptural vessel forms from slabs and fragments of impressed and textured clay. Carved wooden blocks from India, originally for printing textiles, are her most used texture-making implements. Lara throws thin slabs of clay or porcelain onto these textured wooden blocks, and then peels them off. If pressed into the clay, the block

A selection of objects used by Lara Scobie to create textured surfaces.

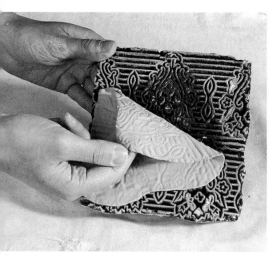

A thin slab of porcelain being removed from a textured wooden block.

is inclined to stick and the resulting image is not as defined or as deeply impressed. By throwing the slab on one way, then turning it and repeating the process, a more complex and less literal pattern is created. Lara does not want the images from the blocks to be readily recognisable as specific motifs, and is more interested in achieving variations of texture. To this end she uses only part of the blocks to achieve the required effects. She aims to create a surface built up of layers of texture, which may have distinguishable elements, but which have somehow metamorphosed into new and different shapes.

The sequence of photographs shows some of the stages involved in building one of Lara's vessels. The initial oval-shaped structure is made from two slabs joined together to which fragments of textured clay are applied. To begin with, the vessel is built upside down. Tubes of clay, made from very thin textured slabs which have been rolled up, are attached one by one, until the entire bottom opening has been covered. Once this base section has stiffened, the piece is turned the right way up. The rim or top of the slabs are then cut irregularly. Many more textured tubes, strips and fragments of clay are added, until the entire surface has been covered in overlapping layers of texture. The cut rim is concealed with strips and quills of clay, which extend over the edge and into the interior of the vessel. In addition to the wooden printing blocks, a variety of objects are used to create different textures including a wooden (meat tenderising) mallet, a metal mechanical cog and a metal toothed comb.

Lara uses a white stoneware clay for

Attaching hollow tubes of textured clay to form the base of the vessel.

some of her pieces and porcelain for others. After biscuit firing, oxides and underglaze colours are applied in washes and then gently sponged off, leaving a residue in the crevices. Colours are built up in layers and once completed, a large Chinese brush which has been dipped into transparent glaze, is drawn across the surface of the vessel. This helps to lift the surface and gives it a gentle sparkle. The pieces are fired to 1260°C in a reduction atmosphere in a gas-fired kiln. Of her work Lara says,

Cutting the rim to shape. *Photographs by Paul Adair.*

Below
Vessel by Lara Scobie (UK), 42 × 20 × 17 cm. Several different techniques were used to create the range of textures on this piece. Porcelain. *Photograph by John McKenzie.*

> My pots are constructed through complex layers of textured and patterned clay. This to me is a fundamental aspect of my work, and it is though experimentation and investigation of manipulating the clay, that the pots have evolved. The texture is the innovator for the form.

Regarding the inspiration for her work, Lara continues,

It is so very hard to pinpoint one single source of inspiration. In fact, so much of what I look at around me every day contributes to my work. However, Chinese bronzes and ancient metal work have always been a wonderful source of inspiration to me. For example, the thin worn edges on some of the Neolithic urns and cooking vessels led me to use the clay as thinly as I do. African adornment has also been a fascinating Art Form for me, and has contributed to my ideas for binding and strapping. But most important is my own individual response to the medium. This has always been a very important aspect for me and something that I shall never underestimate. My pure enjoyment of the clay is something that I cherish, and it would be a great worry for me, if I were to lose this enthusiasm for the material.

As was seen in the chapter on the use of Stamps, Maureen Minchin uses various techniques to create textures in her work. Lengths of wood, nuts and bolts and sprigs made in moulds are used in addition to fired clay stamps to entirely cover the surfaces of her pieces, creating a rich tapestry of textures. (See the photographs in Chapter 3 on stamps.)

It is clear from the work of these two ceramicists that there is more to making successful pieces which have various textures covering the entire surfaces than just filling blank areas on an already completed form, using a variety of texture-making techniques. The textures are not incidental but are integral to the forms, and their use is carefully considered in relation to the finished pieces.

Chapter Ten
Using Two or More Techniques

This chapter is about using a combination of different impressed techniques on single pieces of work.

History

As can be seen from several of the photographs of historical pots included in this book, there have been many periods in the history of pottery where pieces were produced combining a number of different decorating techniques.

Current practices

Nearly all of the contemporary potters whose work is featured in this book combine a number of different methods to mark and texture the surfaces of their work. With some, the different techniques used are not easily distinguishable, whereas in the work of others, there is a clear demarcation between the different methods of decoration used. While some potters may be principally associated with a particular type of impressed decoration, they are likely to use several others as well, to a greater or lesser extent. It is as though an interest in and a liking for textured surfaces encourages continuous experimentation and exploration of the possibilities.

When I first began considering the various chapters to include in this book the work of Jane Hamlyn immediately came to mind as being appropriate for inclusion in almost every one. Writing about her work in *Ceramics Monthly* (April 1989) Jane wrote,

> I like pots which reveal the material of their making, clay; and the state of clay for which I have a particular fondness is soft – not wet, not sticky, but soft. I love the way soft, plastic clay is so responsive; most of my handles are formed by pressing soft clay with or into various textures: rubber flooring, car mats, bits of wood, etc. I also use roulettes and impressed stamps, and some pots incorporate a wheel-thrown and distorted ring, joined to a slab rolled base textured with embossed wallpaper.

Jane likes the precision of these marks. Also they are very suitable for salt glazing which has the propensity for highlighting raised surface texture. She also likes the way in which a mechanically-produced regular pattern becomes varied and enlivened by the random effects of salt glazing.

Rouletting and stamping are done when the clay is leatherhard. The clay is rolled on the textured surfaces when it is softer. The pots are raw glazed on the interior, then at the bone dry stage, areas of different coloured slips are painted on. Finally, a glaze is brushed onto selected areas.

In descriptions of Jane's work, the terms which reappear time and again are 'richly textured' or 'rich surfaces'. While salt glazing has the effect of picking out and enhancing surface detail, it also has a softening effect on what might otherwise be fairly hard-edged patterns. In Jane's work the very precise marks created as a result of using mechanically-produced patterns are thus softened. The use of slips and glazes on her work also contributes to the softening effect, the smooth and runny edges of areas of slip and glaze providing a contrast with the regular lines of the impressed abstract patterns. In the finished work, we are not instantly aware of separate areas of texture or colour, or how the textures may have been created. Instead our attention is attracted by the strong forms, the overall effect being one of harmony. (See also Chapters 4, 6 and 7 and photographs on pages 47, 48, 54 and the frontispiece.)

Teapot by Jane Hamlyn (UK). Rouletted lines. Pattern on handle and lid knob created by rolling on a textured surface. *Photograph by Haru Sameshima.*

Part 2

Incised

When man first began to 'write', it was by scratching signs on to damp clay using a pointed stick or reed. On the very earliest examples, pictures were drawn (pictographs), but soon stylised representations of objects were incised, using just a few marks to represent each object. Gradually these marks became standardised. Clay Tablet, Jamdat Nasr, Iraq, *c.*3,200–3,000 BC, 11 cm/h. This tablet is written in an early form of the Cuneiform Script; circles and half circles indicate numerals. *Ashmolean Museum, Oxford. (1926.564).*

Chapter Eleven
Incising and Sgraffito

While to incise broadly defined means to cut into, for the purposes of this chapter I am regarding incising as the act of creating a narrow cut or scratch in a clay surface, as opposed to carving, where a larger quantity of clay is removed, to the extent that the form of a pot may be altered. (See Chapter 13.) Sgraffito is included as it involves incising – through an applied layer of slip, which is of a contrasting colour to the body, to expose the clay surface beneath.

History

Amongst the pots which perhaps come to mind most readily when considering incised decoration are those made by the Grotta-Pelos Culture (c.3,200 – 2,800 BC) in the Cyclades. Pottery shapes such as pyxides (boxes), both cylindrical and globular, with slightly domed lids and side

lugs, and collared jars, have incised lines often arranged in herringbone patterns. (See the photograph below.) In some cases these lines were filled with a white chalky substance which made the incised patterns more distinctive.

In the pottery of Early and Middle Bronze Age Cyprus (c.2,700 to 1,650 BC), there is also extensive use of incised decoration. Frequently used patterns include horizontal bands, vertical stripes, zig zags and diamonds (see the photograph on page 71). Again, as with the Cycladic pots, the lines were often filled with a white material to make a contrast against the surface of the pots, which were generally black and/or dark red. Many different shapes of pots exist which have this distinctive type of incised decoration. Pots for every day use include bottles, bowls, jugs and cups. Other, much more complex and elaborate shapes were also made, which were specifically intended as grave goods. These include ring vessels, multi-unit vessels (e.g. jugs with two or more necks), and forms on which miniature vessels, similar in type to the main body, have been attached.

The C Group Culture (c.2,200–1,500 BC) in Lower Nubia produced a range of pottery which has become known as 'polished incised ware'. These pots, mainly round-bottomed bowls, have

Cylindrical Pyxis (Box), Cycladic Islands, in the Aegean Sea, Grotta-Pelos Culture c.3200–2800 BC, 10.5 cm/h. Incised herringbone pattern. *Ashmolean Museum, Oxford. (AE. 435).*

decorated surfaces of contrasting smooth burnished and textured areas, the latter consisting of incised stripes, hatched lines, criss cross or herringbone patterns. It is thought that the motifs were derived from basketwork. Fired to a black or sometimes red colour, the incisions were filled with white pigment to make the pattern stand out.

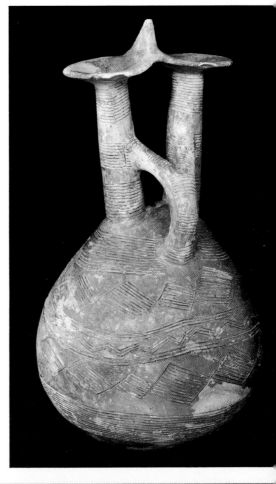

Double-necked Jug, Cyprus, *c.*2,000–1,800 BC, 28.3 cm/h × 15.2 cm/w. Incised decoration. © *The Trustees of the National Museums of Scotland 1996 (1875.43.6).*

Below
Vase and two bowls, Nubia (the ancient land of Nubia, part of the Nile Valley, is today divided between Egypt and the Republic of the Sudan), C-Group Pottery, from Faras (probably early second millennium BC), 15.3 cm/h; 7.6 cm/h; 10.2 cm/h. Vase – impressed diamond pattern; 2 bowls – incised pattern. White pigment was rubbed into the impressed and incised areas to make the pattern stand out against the background. © *The Trustees of the National Museums of Scotland 1996 (1912.319; 1912.531; 1912.532).*

Technique

Incising can be carried out at any time, from when clay is very soft, to when it is almost bone dry. Different effects will be achieved depending on the state of dryness of the clay. Also, different types of tools will be more effective on clay in various stages of dryness. On very soft clay, even blunt instruments can be used successfully to make incised marks. When working on drier clay, it is necessary to

use pointed or sharp tools to achieve a clean cut line. One of the most effective ways of highlighting an incised pattern is to glaze over it with a pale coloured transparent glaze, such as celadon. When this type of glaze is used over a light coloured clay body, the glaze pooling in the incised lines and appearing as a darker shade than the surrounding surface can be very effective. Lines of different depths show as different intensities of the glaze colour.

As regards the sgraffito technique, it is only with practice that you will get to know at what stage of dryness a slip coating is most suitable for incising, depending on the effect you want to

Teapot with Aggressive Spout by Harris Deller (USA), 1994, 24 cm/h × 30.5 cm/w × 7.5 cm/d. Incised cross-hatch pattern. Porcelain.

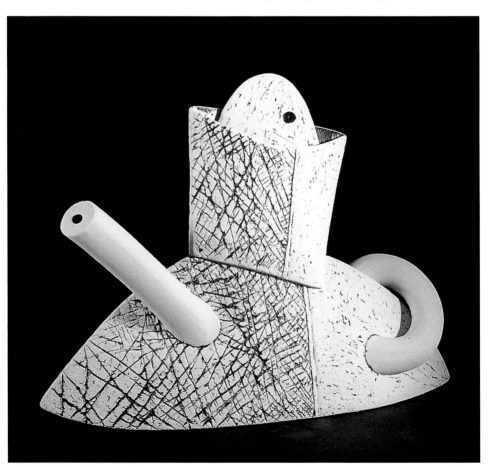

achieve. If the slip is allowed to dry too much, it may flake away at the edges as you cut into it. If the slip is too wet, then it will not be possible to cut precise linear patterns through it. Sgraffito patterns can be most effective when glazed over with a transparent glaze, or on pieces which have a burnished surface, as in the work of Siddig El'nigoumi.

Current practices

Siddig El'nigoumi's pots are made from Fremington clay onto which areas of coloured slips, usually red or grey, are painted. Already at this stage Siddig has in mind the pattern which he will incise through the slip. The pots are allowed to dry to the required state and are then burnished. Siddig uses an assortment of found objects for burnishing, including smooth pebbles, backs of spoons and to get at some difficult areas, an aerial off an old radio. When the burnishing has been completed, Siddig begins to incise the pattern. For this he uses old knitting needles. When working on dishes, they are left in their moulds for support. As he decorates, Siddig rests his hand on a thin

As he incises a pattern on a press moulded dish, Siddig El'nigoumi rests his hand on a narrow piece of wood which spans the mould. *Photograph by Coll Minogue.*

Dish by Siddig El'nigoumi (Sudan/UK), 1994.
Sgraffito decoration. Earthenware. Press
moulded. *Photograph by Coll Minogue.*

piece of wood which spans the mould.
(See photograph on page 73.) Many of his
dishes have intricate geometric patterns
around the border with a single image,
often a fish or a geometric symbol in the
centre. There is always a tiny scorpion,
Siddig's signature, to be found somewhere
in the midst of the pattern on each piece.
The decorated pots are fired to 800°C. The
inspiration for Siddig's work comes from a
wide range of influences: Arab, African
and British. An early training in
calligraphy in his native Sudan is evident
in many pieces. Siddig has lived in Britain
since the late 1960s and over the years

he has used images in his work which are
inspired by what he sees around him or
by events which make an impact on him.
One series of dishes had imagery relating
to the Campaign for Nuclear Disarmanent
(CND) and Greenham Common. Another
series was based on crossword puzzles.
Often ancient Arabic calligraphy is used
in combination with images which come
from Britain in the 1990s to make
somewhat wry commentary on current
affairs.

American ceramicist Harris Deller
makes flattened porcelain pieces, with
intricate linear patterns, which almost
appear to be two-dimensional. These
pieces are initially thrown and while still
wet they are manipulated and

compressed to suppress the volume, distorted and added to, with slabs and coils. As the pieces dry, further refining of the shapes takes place. Extruded handles and spouts are attached to teapots. When the pieces have dried, they are smoothed with a metal rib. Then patterns comprising arcs, stripes or crosshatching are incised using a sharpened stylus, made from a length of brazing rod. Looped tools are used to create lines on large pieces. Harris explains that,

> The work may be incised when the clay is somewhere between leatherhard and bone dry. The dampness of the clay will affect the quality of line I can achieve. I usually begin incising when the piece is leatherhard so I can take advantage of the drying process.

After a biscuit firing, the porcelain pieces are glazed with a black glaze. Excess glaze is then sponged off, leaving a heavy concentration in the incised lines. Next the forms are sanded with coarse sandpaper to preserve the black and white contrast. They are fired to cone 10 in a reduction atmosphere for hardness and brightness. Some pieces are then sandblasted. The result is a range of striking Black and White forms, which at a glance appear to be familiar functional objects – cups and saucers, vases, teapots – but which on further inspection are found to be illusions of these objects. This sense of illusion is strengthened by the linear surface patterns, which serve to camouflage the basic shapes. Harris writes about his work and influences as follows,

> I try to work intuitively very much like a potter. One piece or shape suggesting another; looking for relationships of shape and surface that have the

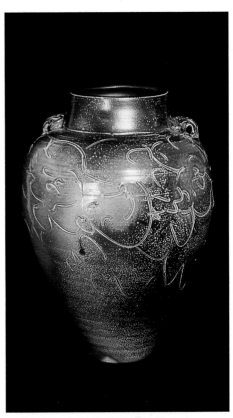

Jar by Janet Mansfield (Aus.), 48 cm/h. Pattern incised through applied slip. Stoneware. Wood-fired salt glaze.

> potential to work. I rely on both refinement and nuance to achieve my best results. My work has been influenced by 'Cycladic' figurines as well as the works of Hans Coper and Lucie Rie.

Salt-glaze potter Sarah Walton (UK) made extensive use of lines incised through slip to decorate her pots throughout the early and mid-1980s. These linear patterns seem particularly compatible with the quiet but rich surface qualities which Sarah achieved in her salt-glazed work at this time. Thrown lidded jars, teapots, jugs, vases and hand-built flower bricks were made, the entire

Large Vase by Sarah Walton (UK). 1981 37.5 cm/h. Diagonal sgraffito decoration. Salt-glazed stoneware.

surface of some, covered with incised lines. Writing about the inspiration for this work, in the Aberystwyth Arts Centre's Ceramic Series (No. 14), Sarah wrote

... it was the folds of garments as they undulated and hung over torsos and limbs and the way crinkled hair fell over shoulders and down Archaic Greek backs that started me off on that path. The direct connection between the figure beneath and the consequent behaviour of the garments over it set me a goal for my forms and the decoration on them.

Australian salt-glaze and wood-fire potter Janet Mansfield (see also Chapter 5) often decorates her work with incised patterns. Lines are incised through applied slip using a wedge-shaped

Accessory Cups, East Lothian (Lt.) and Orkney (Rt.), Scotland, c.1900–1500 BC, 6.5 cm/h and 6.8 cm/h. Incised decoration. © *The Trustees of the National Museums of Scotland 1996 (EC 4, Lt., EC 1 Rt.).* Also, see photograph on page 109.

applied slip using a wedge-shaped wooden tool to achieve a variety of marks – wide, narrow, deep, shallow. These linear patterns are accentuated by being salt-glazed.

From the work of these four potters, we see how incising can be successfully employed in the creation of very different styles of work, ranging from low-fired sgraffito patterns to salt-glazed stoneware and high-fired porcelain. The range of their work confirms incising as a versatile technique, which can be used and interpreted in many different ways.

Chapter Twelve
Combing

Combing, in the context of this chapter, is using a toothed or pronged instrument to score parallel lines, either directly into a clay surface or through a coating of slip.

History

As combing is one of the most direct methods of decorating a clay surface, it is not surprising that it is to be found on pottery from many different countries and periods. Some fragments of the earliest Nubian pottery of the Khartoum Mesolithic Culture (dating from *c.*6,000 BC) show decoration of wavy incised lines. It is thought that fish bones were used to create these lines. The fragments are from unpainted, hand-built, globular vessels.

In Japan, combing was used on Sueki Ware which was first made around AD400. These mole-grey coloured, wheel-thrown, and high-fired (1,000–1,200°C) pots were unlike any which had previously been made in Japan. Typical of Sueki Ware are multi-mouthed vessels, with animal ornaments, on high or low stands, which often have triangular and rectangular cut-out sections.

In Chinese Celadon Ware, made during the Northern Song Dynasty (AD960–1126), combing was widely used in combination with incising and carving in the decoration of pots. On the piece in the photograph on page 79 (a covered jar

with six cylindrical spouts on the shoulder), the body has three distinct bands of decoration, all comprising of abstract foliage scroll patterns, with carved/incised outlines, which have been filled in with areas of combing. The lid, which is surmounted by a modelled bird,

Vase, Sueki Ware, Japan, 31.8 cm/h 15.2 cm/dia. Bands of combed decoration.
© *The Trustees of the National Museums of Scotland 1996 (1908.392.3).*

also has combed lines. The delicate incising and combing are emphasised and enhanced by the pooling of the celadon glaze.

Combing was used extensively on Medieval English pottery. Patterns include horizontal bands which encircle jugs; combed lines running vertically from rim to base, and combed lines defining rectangular and triangular areas. These decorative features were used in combination with techniques such as rouletting (notched patterns), frilled applied strips of clay, applied pellets of clay, stab marks and thumbed bases.

In areas of Nigeria (middle Niger region), traditional potters use a technique whereby pieces of strong grass held between the fingers are used as a comb, to incise bands of parallel lines on pots. Combs which have been wrapped in a leaf in such a way that only the tips of the teeth protrude are used by potters of the Ibibio tribe to make combed lines, especially around the necks of jars.

In many of the islands in the Milne Bay Province of Papua New Guinea, combing is widely used in the decoration of traditional round-bottomed cooking pots. On one island, pots are decorated with parallel wavy lines using two, three or four pronged combs, made from black palm wood. On another island combs made from sago palm bark or mid-rib, with between two and six prongs, are used as decorating tools. In making these combs the teeth are levelled off by holding them briefly against a glowing ember.

Technique

A comb which can be any toothed instrument, when drawn through clay or slip, produces parallel lines, and is perhaps most effective when used to make wavy parallel lines. For combing through

Lidded vase, China, Northern Song Dynasty, AD 960–1126. Celadon glaze over incised and combed decoration. Stoneware. *Glasgow Museums: The Burrell Collections (38/286).*

slip, a comb can be made using any pliable material, such as cardboard or plastic. For making incised combed lines in clay, a harder material needs to be used. Many found objects are suitable – plastic or metal forks, the ends of wooden sections from honey combs, parts of old saw blades etc. The rectangular pieces of hard plastic with serrated edges, which are provided for spreading many types of thick adhesives, are ideally suited as ready-made 'combs' for use on clay

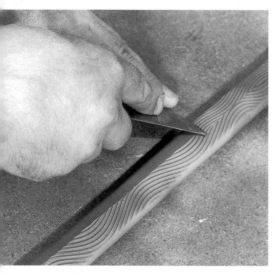

A wallpaper remover with a serrated edge is used to create flowing wavy lines on a strap handle.

surfaces. Each of these examples will make different types of lines. If no ready-made comb is available, or if it is not possible to create the required quality of line with any that are available, it is fairly easy to make a comb. One of the easiest materials to use is a thin piece of wood approximately 3 mm thick, and long enough to be held comfortably when in use. Decide on the number of teeth you want and the size of the spaces between the teeth, then, using a narrow file or a saw, cut grooves in the end edge of the wood to create the desired effect. If the teeth are too close together, the comb will quickly become clogged with clay. It is best to wait until the rough edges, created by combing through leatherhard clay, are dry before cleaning them up, or the combed lines may become smudged. Combs for combing through slip generally have flat-topped rather than pointed teeth, and teeth which are not very close together. Combed slip decoration is most effective, as are other slip decorating techniques such as sgraffito, when the

slip used is of a contrasting colour to the clay body beneath.

Current practices

British salt-glaze potter Richard Dewar, who has lived and worked in France since 1979, uses an assortment of tools and a variety of techniques to create a wide range of textures on his work. Commenting on his use of tools, Richard says 'The tools I use are fairly basic. Potters are renowned as being ace scavengers in house and kitchen and my selection of pottery tools tends to echo

Rectangular Bottle by Geoff Crispin (Aus.). 29 cm/h. Combed and carved decoration under a celadon glaze. Slipcast porcelain. Wood-fired.

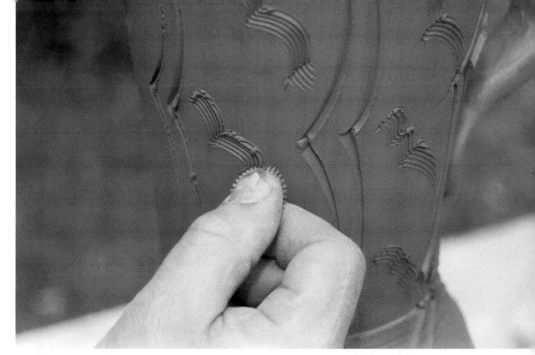

Combed lines are made with the edge of a small cog wheel.

Right
An overall pattern is built up from a variety of combed lines.

this.' Included are a serrated wallpaper remover, a hacksaw blade, serrated plastic bits gleaned from the cutter in a 'cling film' box, part of a plastic hair comb and a cog from a child's clockwork toy, all of which are used to make combed marks. His method of working is as follows. Having thrown a basic jug shape, a lip is attached. The serrated wallpaper remover is used to make flowing wavy lines on the strap handle before it is attached. Then the decoration process begins. The bottom section of the pot is cut to create facets, using a stretched spiral curtain wire, which creates a textured surface of wavy lines. Next, using the point of a filed off hacksaw blade, vertical lines are incised in the top portion of the jug form, outlining areas for further decoration. Using an

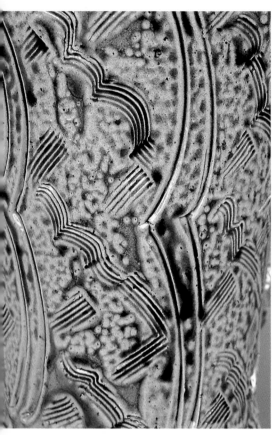

Detail of Jug by Richard Dewar (UK/France). Combed and incised decoration. Salt-glazed stoneware.

the result he wants to achieve, then he finds a way of achieving it through various methods of surface decoration.

Another potter who uses combing in his work is Australian Geoff Crispin. Much of Geoff's work is slipcast. He describes his working method as follows,

I make a model out of plaster and then make one mould using that model. The cast that comes out of the mould is a blank with no decoration. As soon as the cast is hard enough to handle without damage or distortion, the carving is carried out. The combing is the last process and is usually done at an angle, to accentuate the movement of the decoration around the pot.

The tools Geoff uses for combing are small pieces of hacksaw blade. Several sizes are used depending on the surface to be combed.

The pots are bisque fired and then glazed. Because of all the carving and combing, a thin wash of glaze is first painted all over the pot before it is dipped. If this is not done, small pockets of air can be trapped when the pot is dipped. This leads to pinholing in the fired glaze. When the glaze is dry, all glaze runs are smoothed over. The pots are then wood-fired.

The relatively simple action of combing through a coating of slip, to reveal parallel wavy lines of a contrasting colour, can completely enliven a clay surface. Equally, combing directly into clay, a series of zig zag, curved or straight lines, can be a very effective decorating technique, especially when combined with glazes which emphasise the pattern, such as a transparent or translucent glaze, or when the work is salt-glazed.

assortment of tools (see above) several combed lines are made on the clay surface, some straight, some V-shaped, others undulating, until an all over pattern is built up. Richard considers that incised and impressed decorating techniques, especially '. . . combing and cutting really come into their own when used in combination with salt-glazing. The effect of the vapour glaze on any raised edge, will search out the relief and give it emphasis.' Before he begins to decorate a pot, Richard has an image of

Chapter Thirteen
Carving

Here I am taking the term 'to carve' as meaning to cut into, to remove a quantity of clay, as opposed to incise. Carving, whether low or high relief, has more of an impact on the surface and form of a piece than incising. As fluting involves the cutting or carving of grooves (flute – a longitudinal groove), it is included in this chapter.

Beaker, Japan, Jomon Period, 15.2 cm/h 15.2 cm/dia. Carved/Incised decoration. © *The Trustees of the National Museums of Scotland 1996 (1909.500.142).*

History

Many of the pots made during the Jomon period in Japan have textured carved surfaces. Some have areas of rolled cord decoration bordered by deep grooves, carved/cut from the clay surface. On others, additional decoration in the form of ridges (some known as 'cake decoration' style, others as 'macaroni' style) has been applied to the surface of pots, thus creating three different surface levels, and heightening the overall impact of the decoration, through the interplay of light and shade.

Many consider that carving and fluting as decorative techniques reached a peak in the celadon wares produced during the Chinese Song Dynasty (AD960–1279). The sensitive and rhythmically carved patterns, often based on flowers, particularly the lotus and the peony, foliage and scenes from nature, have a wonderful flowing quality. Carved lines were bevelled in such a way that the glaze covering the pattern, darkened as depth increased (see photograph on page 79). In addition to these pieces with elaborate carved patterns, some pots, notably bowls, were produced which have a simple carved design based on the lotus leaf around the outside. (See photograph on page 84). The blue green celadon glaze used on these pieces is reminiscent of jade in both colour and texture.

One type of traditional pottery made in the East Sepik Province of Papua New

Guinea has the appearance of very dark carved and polished wood. The pots, many of which are conical shaped eating bowls or large serving bowls, are made by coiling and have carved designs, often including curved, grooved lines. The patterns are carved and gouged, using tools fashioned from wild betel nuts. The pots are burnished, both inside and outside to a high gloss, using the rounded back edge of a bamboo knife, the burnished surface creating a distinct contrast with the carved areas.

Technique

Depending on the state of dryness of clay, carving can be carried out using a wide variety of tools. Soft clay can be carved with any type of wire loop tool. When leatherhard, it is necessary to use sharper

Bowl, China, Southern Song Dynasty, AD 1127–1279 16.5 cm/dia. Carved lotus design under Longquan type celadon glaze. Porcelain. *Glasgow Museums: The Burrell Collection (38/299).*

tools to remove the clay e.g. a filed off piece of hacksaw blade. Carving is often the first stage involved in inlaid decoration. (See Chapter 14 on Inlay).

Fluted decoration generally involves the cutting of well-defined, clean lines which often follow and accentuate the form of a pot. Depending on the tool being used and the angle at which it is held, the cross section of an individual 'flute' can vary from a cut which has one perpendicular and one sloped side, to a V-shaped cut which leaves a pointed, inverted V-shaped ridge between cuts, or round-bottomed grooves with straight or sloped sides. When throwing pots which are to be fluted, it is important to keep in mind the depth of the flutes, and to make the walls of the pot of a corresponding thickness. Clay is at its most suitable for fluting when it is leatherhard. Translucent glazes are particularly effective over fluted decoration. As the glaze pools and appears darker in the depth of the grooves, and becomes paler on the ridges in between, the linear pattern is very much accentuated.

Current practices

Antonia Salmon (UK) uses the technique of carving on some of her burnished and sawdust-fired forms. Some pieces are thrown, while others are hand-built using flattened coils. Once the form is finished, the positions of horizontal bands are marked using a pencil. Then lines are scored with a metal stylus. Next, alternate bands are gouged out with a looped tool. The raised bands are initially burnished using the back of a teaspoon. These areas will be burnished three or four times in all. The bands in between the burnished areas are combed and textured, using a metal kidney with a serrated edge. Antonia says of this work,

I use this decoration technique because the smooth burnished surface works very well with the subtle texturing. There is a gentle contrast in surfaces. My work has a very tactile finish and by incising or texturing the surface there is a new dimension of interest. The patterns are influenced from assimilating information about prehistoric, Celtic and South American patterning. The patterns are rarely pre-planned.

Clay is removed using a wire looped tool.

Raised areas are burnished using the back of a teaspoon.

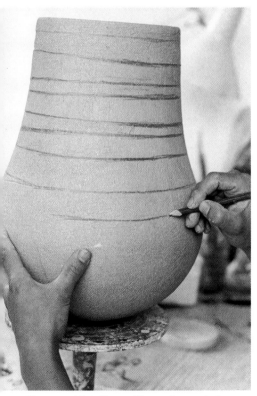

Lines marking the positions of areas to be carved are drawn in pencil on the surface of the hand-built form.

Antonia uses a fine white stoneware clay. Her work is bisque fired to 1060°C, prior to firing in sawdust, over a period of 24 hours. Finally, each piece is wax polished which imparts a soft glow. In an article in *Ceramic Review* (Number 130, 1990) Antonia wrote,

> When I think of work which has inspired me, it is often anonymous ethnic pieces or those of ancient origin whose feeling of purpose and freshness has survived the centuries. I am thinking of small items such as farming implements, combs, stools, mirrors, wristbands, whose forms are uniquely related to function and whose craftsmanship is to be cherished for its dignity.

American potter Lynne Crumpacker makes pots which are intended for use, but are extensively altered and carved after the initial throwing stage. She describes her reasons for doing this as follows: 'I've come to the conclusion that the primal reason that makes me want to carve, stamp, alter in some fashion comes from the clay itself! There is something astounding about taking soft, malleable clay and turning it into a hard permanent form . . .'. In carving and altering her work Lynne uses very simple tools – a kitchen knife, a wood knife, flat metal tools. Altering the pots starts on the

A selection of the tools Antonia Salmon uses when making her hand-built, carved and burnished pieces.

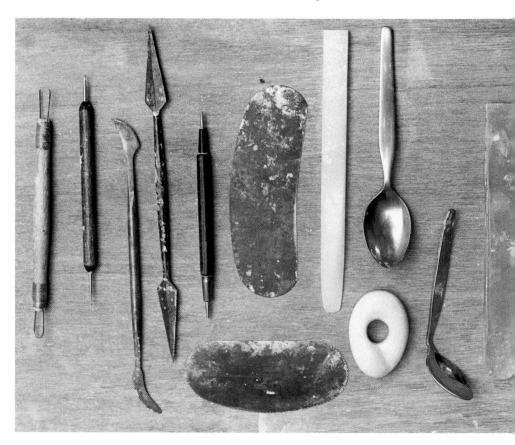

Pot with horizontal texture by Antonia Salmon (UK), 1988. Hand-built, carved, textured, burnished and sawdust-fired. Stoneware.

wheel, pushing out from the inside or pushing in from the outside. Further alteration takes place as the clay dries. Detailed carving is done at the leatherhard stage. Lynne is particularly inspired by pottery from the Early Jomon period.

Large-scale clay work, in a leatherhard state or drier, can be carved in a way similar to that in which other, harder materials are carved. American artist Arnold Zimmerman creates monumental carved sculptural pieces in clay. He writes,

My work is influenced by art and architecture from many different cultures, in many different time periods. The carving of the clay walls springs directly from the ongoing dialogue I've had with the material dating back 25 years, when I trained as a potter in England and the US. I no longer make functional pottery but

still retain and utilise the experience of that craft in my sculpture. My forms are built up first and are hollow; then carved, added on to, carved some more etc. So it is additive and subtractive at the same time. Also these pieces are glazed. It's a different manipulation of the age old ceramic process.

Many of the pieces Arnold creates in this way measure up to two metres or more in height.

Carlos van Reigersberg-Versluys (UK) makes individual pieces with intricately worked surfaces. Original influences were African pots, particularly those made by the Ibo and other Nigerian tribes. The pieces are worked on while the clay is still soft. Until recently most of the carving was done using various wire loop tools. Now Carlos uses a technique which is perhaps best described as displacing clay rather than carving. The rounded tip of a wooden modelling tool is pushed into the clay, and drawn through it to make the required shape. As the clay is soft and the tool blunt, the clay in the path of the tool rises in ridges at both sides. Thus grooves are formed with raised edges, creating three surface levels on the pieces. Carlos uses a buff stoneware clay to which grog and fire clay are added. The pieces are glazed either in a dry barium glaze or a matt ash glaze (see page 90).

Derek Emms (UK) uses the techniques of fluting and carving on his stoneware and porcelain pots. He has always liked

Left
Jug by Lynne Crumpacker (USA), 35.5 cm/h. Thrown, with hand-built parts. Carved decoration.

Right
Columns by Arnold Zimmerman (USA), 1989, 305/h × 71 to 101 cm. Carved stoneware.

Bowl by Carlos van Reigersberg-Versluys (UK), 15 cm/h. The clay is carved or incised using blunt wooden tools whilst it is still soft. Stoneware matt ash glaze.

Chinese and Korean celadon wares and considers that this must have subconsciously influenced his work. His pots are carved at the leatherhard stage using homemade loop tools – triangular for sharp edges, U-shaped for shallow round flutes and round for larger round flutes. For angular fluting he uses a sharpened piece of hacksaw blade. The decoration, whether carved or fluted, is beautifully enhanced by the range of glazes which Derek uses (mostly celadon or tenmoku), each line and shape emphasised by the slight pooling of glaze.

The combined work of the five ceramicists, whose techniques are briefly described here, illustrates how carving and fluting can be employed in the creation of an incredibly wide range of ceramics.

Teapot by Derek Emms (UK). Carved decoration under celadon glaze. Porcelain.

Chapter Fourteen
Inlaying

Inlaying is the technique whereby shallow depressions made either by impressing or removing areas of a clay surface are filled in with a clay or slip of a contrasting colour. The surface is later levelled off by scraping away the excess to reveal the clearly defined pattern.

Bowl, Korean, Koryo Dynasty, AD 935–1392, 6.7/h × 20 cm/dia. Celadon glaze over inlaid decoration. Stoneware. *Glasgow Museums: The Burrell Collection (38/346).*

History

Probably the best known historical pottery with inlaid decoration is that made during the Koryo Dynasty (*c.* AD 935–1,392) in Korea. This pottery has inlaid patterns in white and black, under a grey-green celadon glaze. (See photograph below.) Patterns were generally inspired by nature and included flowers such as chrysanthemums and lotuses, storks, clouds, willow trees etc.

The shapes to be inlaid were carved out and filled with black or white slip. In some instances repeat patterns were created by pressing in stamps made of wood, fired clay or the ends of bamboo sticks, which were either left plain to impress circles, or notched to create various patterns. In the Yi Dynasty, which followed on from the Koryo Dynasty, inlaid wares continued to be produced, but these were generally of a very different style. Instead of carving designs, many pots were decorated with all over stamped patterns of mesh, hatching or flower heads, over which a white slip was brushed. The excess slip was wiped off leaving a residue in the impressions created by the stamps. The Japanese term 'Mishima' is now commonly used not only to describe these Korean inlaid wares, but also the technique of inlaying in general.

As we have seen in earlier chapters, the incised patterns on many prehistoric pots were often filled with white materials with the purpose of making the patterns stand out, by creating a greater contrast against the background colour of the pots. These include pots made during the Bronze Age in the Cyclades (3,200–2,200 BC); Cypriot pottery of the Early and Middle Bronze Age (2,700–1,650 BC) and the polished incised ware made by the C Group culture in Nubia (2,200–1,500 BC). There is evidence that some Neolithic beakers, both in Britain and Europe, had their impressed – comb tooth – patterns, enhanced by filling with a white paste. This paste contained crushed burnt bone in some examples and crushed chalk fossils in others.

Technique

Some of the techniques already described in previous chapters can be considered as preliminary stages for inlaying. These include stamps, roulettes and rolled cord. Patterns made using other techniques could also be considered as appropriate for inlaying – impressions made by repeatedly pressing in natural or manmade objects for instance. However I am concerned here with inlay following the removal of material by incising, combing or carving, rather than in hollows made by impressing. The following descriptions of different methods of inlaying patterns, using both coloured slip and clay, contain instructions and helpful advice on various aspects of the technique.

Current practices

Lex Dickson is an Australian potter who frequently uses inlaid decoration in his work (see photograph on page 94). When pots are ready for decorating, first the intended pattern is marked out. The horizontal lines are incised with the pot on the wheel and then the remainder of the pattern is carved out. The first layer of slip is applied using a soft brush, ensuring that air bubbling does not occur. Subsequent layers of slip are then applied, usually a total of four or five in all, and allowed to dry to leatherhard consistency between coats. It is important that the pot is not allowed to dry out too much between applications of slip. Carelessness in this aspect of the technique will result in the slip cracking away from the body clay. Once all the coats of slip have been applied and the last coat has dried, the slip is at first cut back roughly to reveal the inlaid pattern underneath. Then the slip is cut back very carefully to complete the process, while making sure that none of the surface of the pot is removed. After biscuit firing, the pots are sprayed with a thin coating of wood ash or nepheline syenite glaze, and fired to between 1280° and 1300°C. The clay which Lex predominantly uses is a dark, iron speck-free, stoneware. The patterns are inlaid with slip made from a white stoneware. The technique can be reversed by inlaying white stoneware with darker coloured slip. The slip can be coloured by adding oxides or stains. Lex writes of his work,

> My interest in the slip inlay technique developed through my study of Korean pots of the Yi and Koryo Dynasties. The fact that the decoration on these pots could be intricate, while at the same time retaining subtle qualities, appealed to me. For many years I have been interested in geometry, and this together with a keen interest in pots of indigenous potters of many countries, i.e. Africa and New Guinea, lent itself to this form of decoration. I particularly like the way some element of the environment is depicted in simple geometric patterns by these early potters. This remains a strong influence on my work.

American artist David Roesler also uses inlay in his work. The sculptural forms he constructs from slabs of red earthenware clay have a broad range of surface patterns and colours, with as many as six colours inlaid separately. Some vessel forms have curved or pointed bases and rest on specially constructed stands (see photograph on page 95). In addition, many have stoppers which, when removed, reveal further inlaid patterns on the interior. David states one of the reasons for his use of inlay as follows, 'This method allows me to work for the greatest amount of time on the piece while it is leatherhard, my favourite stage of the ceramic process'. (See photograph sequence on pages 96 and 97.)

Carving for the first colour to be inlaid begins after the form has dried to a leatherhard stage. David then continues carving using various homemade tools including carving sticks, some pointed, or with triangular ends etc. Dots of various sizes are made with drill bits carefully twirled in his fingers. To clear away crumbs in the carved area, before applying the slip, an artist's oil painting brush is sometimes used. It is slightly stiff, but does not damage the carving. The first colour of slip is brushed into the carved areas. Several coats may be necessary to fill them completely. The piece is wrapped in plastic until the slip has firmed to leatherhard. Once the slip and clay body are of the same firmness, scraping begins. For scraping, a one-edged razor blade or metal rib is used for convex and flat surfaces, and a round razor blade for concave surfaces (the interiors of bowls etc.). The process is repeated for the other colours. Each time the piece is scraped, any residual slip from previous colours is removed too. Care must be taken not to scrape too much, or previously inlaid areas might also be scraped away.

After inlaying is finished and the piece has dried to bone dry, David sometimes cleans the surface with fine steel wool. He points out that a dust mask is absolutely necessary for this step. Then the piece is biscuit fired to cone 04–05. After biscuit firing, underglaze colours are applied to some pieces to create larger areas of colour and to achieve an interesting depth of detail on a smooth surface. The work is brushed with a transparent satin, or clear gloss glaze, and fired to cone 05–06. The use of satin glaze gives a finished piece which most closely resembles its leatherhard predecessor. David stresses that one of the most important things about doing 'Mishima'

Platter by Lex Dickson, (Aus.), 38 cm/dia.
Stoneware, inlaid with white stoneware slip.
Wood ash and tenmoku glaze.

is the smoothness of the clay body. Even
one grain of grog/sand can scar the
surface and pattern when the scraping is
done. After much experimentation, he
now uses a red earthenware body that is
dry screened by hand before mixing and
pugging. David Roesler's work well
illustrates how a traditional technique
such as 'Mishima', can be re-interpreted
creatively and employed in the
production of contemporary ceramic art.

Jutka Fischer is another potter who
makes use of the inlay technique, but
instead of brushing in slip, coloured clays
are inlaid. A white earthenware clay body
is allowed to dry and is then powdered
and mixed with body stains to make up
different coloured clays. Slabs of these
clays are rolled out and joined together to
make large patchwork slabs, which are
used to hand-build a range of
asymmetrically shaped pots. Sometimes
the slabs of clay are used to line plaster
moulds for bowls or dishes and are joined
together in the mould. Handles and
spouts are attached to the pots when the
clay is leatherhard. Designs are then

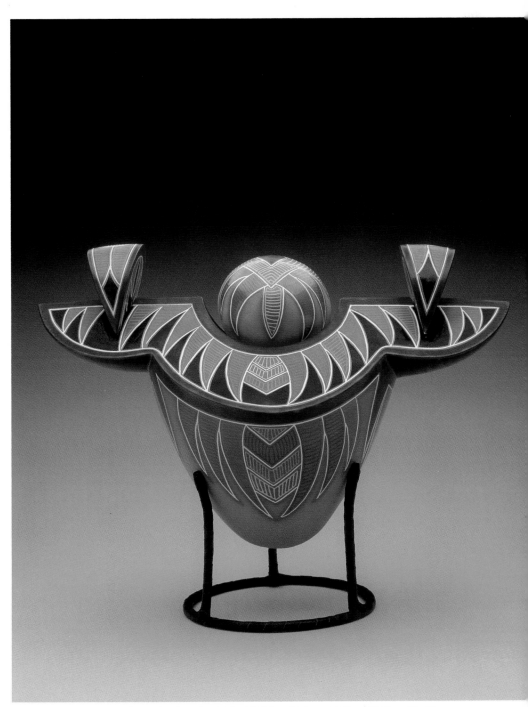

'Balled Victory' by David Roesler (USA), 1992, 45.5/h × 53/w × 30.5 cm/d. Hand-built earthenware. Mishima, underglaze colours, clear satin glaze. On a stand of steel and leather. *Photograph by Gary Garnick. From a Private Collection, Los Angeles, California.*

Above
David Roesler carves out the areas to be inlaid with the first colour of slip.

Below
The first colour of slip is brushed into the carved areas.

Above
Excess slip is scraped away using a one-edged razor blade.

Below
The processes of carving, brushing in slip and removing excess slip are repeated until the pattern comprised of several different colours is completed. *Photographs by Brad Fowler.*

'Two vases with birds and fish' by Jutka Fischer (UK). Formed from slabs of coloured clay, inlaid. Additional decoration applied with underglaze colours, pencils and crayons. Earthenware.

drawn on each of the areas of coloured clay. Next these shapes are carved out to a depth of about half the thickness of the slab. Clays of contrasting colours are pressed into the hollows and the pot, covered in polythene, is left overnight so that the soft inlaid clay has an opportunity to stiffen. The next day excess clay is scraped off and further inlaying takes place. Depending on the complexity of the design, pots can take three or four days to complete. They are allowed to dry out very slowly over a period of about two weeks. The surface is then given a final cleaning by sanding with fine grade wire wool. The work is biscuit fired to 1060°C and then glazed on the inside with a clear glaze. Underglaze colours, pencils and crayons are used to apply fine details, which add depth to the otherwise flat effect of the inlaying. Next the

outsides of the pots are sprayed with a soft transparent alumina matt glaze, after which they are fired to 1000°C. Jutka comments on her work, 'When the thickness of glaze and firing temperature are just right, the effect is a satiny smooth surface, with a soft sheen – not unlike glazed cotton fabric'.

Both Mick and Sheila Casson have in the past made pieces with inlaid decoration. Sheila's work was in porcelain, often bowls with decoration inspired by landscape. After incising the

Storage jar by Mick Casson (UK), 30.5/h × 30.5 cm/w. Heavy iron-bearing clay body with inlaid pattern of porcellaneous slip, under a dry ash glaze. Stoneware.

pattern at the leatherhard stage, using a porcupine quill, the lines were filled with a thick slip made of the porcelain body with additions of cobalt and iron oxide. Additional decoration was done using paper or latex resist techniques, and spraying oxides. Finally more lines were incised through the coloured areas to reveal the porcelain body beneath.

Mick's inlaid pieces, often large store jars and footed bowls, were made from an iron-bearing body. The pattern was incised using a lollipop stick with a cleft cut into one flattened end, and then inlaid with porcelain (to which about 10% ball clay was added, to help it stay in place). The excess clay was scraped off, then the piece was dipped in a thin slip of 50% china clay, 50% ball clay. This slip was rubbed away to reveal the porcelain inlay and various other selected areas. The pots were glazed with a dry ash glaze and oil-fired to 1280°C. Mick comments on this range of work, 'The technique and aesthetic inspiration all come from one wonderful pot – a Cypriot pot (c.2,000 BC) – hand-built, not thrown'.

The illustrations of pieces by the potters and artists whose working methods are described above are evidence of the very wide range of effects it is possible to achieve using variations of the inlay technique.

Part 3
Personal Expression

Jar with lid, China, Han Dynasty, 206 BC–AD 220. Freely incised pattern of birds, under a feldspathic glaze. High-fired earthenware. *Glasgow Museums: The Burrell Collection (38/48).*

Chapter Fifteen
Gestures in Clay

When a mark is made in clay, it is in itself a record of the action by which it was created. Some marks record slow, deliberate, controlled actions – others are indicative of vigorous, spontaneous gestures. When a mark records a spontaneous gesture, it tells us not only about the physical action by which it was created, but also conveys something of the emotion which was translated into that action.

For some artists, their actions/gestures as they work on each piece, are in themselves an important element of the overall artistic statement.

Neil Tetkowski in his studio.

NEIL TETKOWSKI

Neil Tetkowski is an American ceramic artist who lives in Buffalo in New York State. For many years he experimented with, and was known for, very large thrown disc forms, often up to one metre in diameter, and made from about 136 kg of clay. His studio is in what was once a thriving industrial area with several steel mills. The remnants of that industry, the rundown mills and heavy machinery, are still to be seen there. Gradually the influence of this environment manifested itself in Neil's work. In a body of work entitled 'American Iron and Steel Series', made in 1986, found objects such as cog

wheels, railroad spikes, gears and chains were used to create vigorous incisions and impressed marks on the surfaces of large thrown discs, before some of them were permanently embedded in the clay. This series showed Neil's response to modern life as it has been affected by the Industrial Revolution.

More recently his work has combined ceramics and performance art. At one such event, which took place at the time of the Gulf War, in front of an invited audience, a three-foot disc was thrown, then lowered to the floor. Surrounded by

'Railroad Mandala Series (RMS) #3' by Neil Tetkowski (USA), 1991, 55 cm/diam. This series 'features found objects from the American railroad industry. Each work incorporates four railroad spikes. In the tradition of the Mandala, they are symmetrically arranged in each disc form.' *Photograph by Bruce Mayer.*

performing jazz musicians, Neil proceeded to work on the surface of the disc, his actions in time with the music. Using individual bullets and cartridge belts, the surface of the clay was impressed, combed

Neil Tetkowski at work on a piece created to communicate the artist's response to the Gulf War.

and gouged. The objects used to make the marks were then arranged and embedded in the clay. The completed clay work, titled 'Ground War', was later cast in bronze.

Another body of work, the 'Railroad Mandala Series', features found objects from the American railroad industry. Each work incorporates four railroad spikes (see photograph on page 103). The series included both disc and 'smokestack' forms.

Before firing, the pieces are sprayed with terra sigillata to which colouring oxides have been added. During firing to 960°C, the kiln is lightly salted. In the fired work, the delicate colour variations on the clay surface, often tones of pale blue or pink (achieved by a combination of the use of the terra sigillata and the firing process), are in marked contrast to the harshness of the jagged gouges, incisions and imprints, and more especially the steel objects, some now blackened, which remain embedded in the clay. Neil succeeds in making powerful artistic statements, incorporating found manmade objects selected from his environment, in such a way that the energy and power expended in creating each piece, is clearly recorded in the finished work.

Chapter Sixteen
Drawing in Clay

The plastic nature of clay invites us to manipulate it. A soft or leatherhard clay surface, flat or in the round similarly invites, some would say compels, us to make a mark, to press into, to scratch, to leave some record of ourselves. Drawing in clay using a pointed implement is one of the most direct ways of doing this. While drawings are most often thought of as being flat and made on paper using pencil, drawing in clay – by its very nature – gives another dimension. Even when working on a flat clay slab, a mark is made into the clay and is not just on the surface – it also creates a depth and a shadow. Drawing on thrown or hand-built forms is more complex again, and is not just a matter of wrapping a drawing around a pot and joining it up.

FRANK BOYDEN

This chapter is about the work of Frank Boyden, an American potter and artist, who for several years has concentrated on drawings in clay. The following account, mainly comprised of quotes from Frank, describes in detail the tools he uses, his approach to drawing in clay and comments on how his style of drawing has been directly influenced by the fact that most of his ceramic work is fired in a wood-fired kiln. To begin, Frank describes his use of tools and implements in drawing.

> I've used almost anything that works and I have a huge collection of drawing tools. They are very important and it is necessary to use appropriate tools for different jobs. I have a lot of bones I draw with, of these I use most often a small, pointed, residual bone about 25 cm long from the front leg of a moose. It was given to me by a wonderful old woman in Alaska. I use African porcupine quills because they are light and delicate. I use a variety of sizes and weights of bronze welding rod. I use very hard pencils which I sharpen to pin points, often the pencils are very short, 9-10 cm. I use my fingers, serrated metal ribs, knife blades . . . Each object gives unique marks. Often I feel that a tool which works well to delicately incise soft procelain, does not work very well to incise heavy, hard sculpture clay. It is difficult to make violent incisions with tools which do not fit that purpose. There is a direct relation visually between the tool and the mark it leaves, and I think the way you feel about the tool. I have tools which I have used for years, they have incised thousands of pots. They are my close friends and over time I have discovered how to use them. I believe that anything can and should be used. It all works and all that anyone needs to do is to familiarise themselves with whatever is chosen and they can draw with it. Everything makes a different mark and has a unique line quality.

Writing about drawing on clay in *The Studio Potter* magazine (Volume 14, No. 1) Frank wrote,

Frank Boyden – these two photographs show
stages in creating a very large sculptural
form. This piece was later cast in bronze.

Most of my drawings on clay rely upon
incised lines. Incision is direct and the
clay determines the visual and tactile
qualities of such drawing. Incised lines
are active and since they are hollow,
they are subject to direct interaction
with light. Such interaction makes
shadows, contradicts depth, and can
visually dissolve space and radically
alter form. This direct confrontation of
the clay edges, interior space, and light
has the ability to produce powerful and
animated drawings, an effect not
possible with flat drawings. Incision
has the added advantage of producing
texture, and the lines produced in this

manner expose everything. One
immediately becomes aware of the
edges, the lines, the raised burrs, the
tearing of the clay, and importantly
the texture of the interior of the
material. Such an approach to
drawing also exposes the states that
the clay has passed through as it has
been worked. That is unique. Incision
reveals a great deal about the
draftsman, the sureness of his vision,
and the kinesthetics of the process of
making the particular drawing.

As to whether he has an overall image
in mind before commencing to draw and

on his personal approach to drawing, Frank comments as follows,

> Yes, often I do have an image (general) before I work, however I never draw out on paper any image prior to putting it on a pot. The reason is that it is impossible to transfer a flat image to a round form. There is so much distortion when you drape a flat drawing on a cylinder or a sphere. It is very difficult to make a good drawing to begin with! If you make a drawing on paper which is good and you make it with pencil, it will be impossible to transfer that drawing to a sphere. Clay is the most beautiful material in the world to draw on. Incised drawings are so rich and impart real space, real shadow and real light. These aspects can never be dealt with on a flat piece of paper. I work by making series of

Plate by Frank Boyden (USA), 66 cm/dia. Wood-fired stoneware. *Photograph by Jim Piper.*

pieces, 8–10 pieces. I will then work out a drawing or idea on these pieces. Perhaps I will get one or two out of the kiln.

Inspiration for the imagery used in Frank's work comes from the natural world around his home and studio near the Salmon River Estuary in Oregon. Re-occurring themes in his work include ravens, herons and salmon. Regarding possible influences on his work from historic or prehistoric pottery, artefacts or art, Frank writes,

I was trained as a painter, printmaker and art historian. I think it almost impossible for any work done today not to be so influenced. I am very interested in drawing on round forms and of perceiving drawing in three dimensions (in the round). I am therefore influenced by the drawing on Neolithic Chinese pots, Minoan and Greek work. I am very taken with Nasca pots from Peru as well as contemporary work coming out of the upper Amazon. I use a lot of animal imagery on my work and have looked hard at work that utilises such imagery. Magdalenian painting and especially small bone carving, Chimu ceramics from Peru, Mimbres work from New Mexico and early Zuni work. I am very fond of the tiny ivory carvings made for children of the Inuit depicting all the animals of the Arctic.

Over the past ten years most of Frank's ceramic work has been wood-fired in an Anagama kiln, a fact which has had a direct influence on his style of drawing.

The firing is violent often covering lines and obscuring things. In order to best take advantage of the way the kiln functions, my drawings and incisions have taken on a more violent nature,

often deep and often raising a burr which catches ash. Often the insides of incisions are radically different in colour than the surfaces of the pieces. With the wood-fired porcelains I have often rubbed stains into the incisions so they will show up better. I have used many fine grained porcelains in wood-fired kilns. I have been using Limoges clays from France and Czechoslovakian clays, because the colour is so beautiful. These clays I incise very delicately because I just can not be violent with it. I will often draw from the inside of pieces, pushing the skin of the piece out and using very minimal surface drawing. Pieces of this nature fired in the wood kiln are often very successful, because the rain of ash settles upon all such risings of the surface, and so with care I can use this technique to shade the surface drawing.

Working in clay is just one aspect of Frank's work as an artist. He is also a printmaker, making lithographs, etchings, silkscreen prints, and prints from wet clay slabs. He works in stone, mostly large stones, where he carves or sandblasts drawings into them. Many such pieces are used in landscape designs and with architecture. In the past seven years he has also worked in cast bronze. This came about because of his desire to work on a large scale, while avoiding the immense problems, both technical and visual, of working large scale with clay. He found that he could transfer all the best qualities of clay to metal, and easily achieve wonderful colour and incredible durability. The scale was the most important aspect of the decision to extend work into this medium. It has allowed him to explore many areas which he could not deal with, with clay alone.

End Piece

The range of work illustrated and described in the preceding chapters is indicative of the versatility of Impressing and Incising, and the scope for personal expression which is possible using these fundamental techniques.

As has been seen, these techniques are appropriate for use with many different methods of glazing and firing. Impressed and incised marks can be the first level in building up complex effects, involving coloured slips and multiple layers of glaze. Equally, they can form the basis of very quiet pieces, where the only additional embellishments to the clay surface are the flame markings and natural ash glaze which result from high temperature wood-firing.

While some contemporary ceramicists use the techniques of impressing and incising in combination with the most modern of ceramic materials, others are using techniques little changed from prehistoric times. As ceramic technology advances further and develops ever new methods and materials for colouring and decorating clay surfaces, on the strength and diversity of the work currently being produced using Impressed and Incised techniques, it is likely that the immediacy and spontaneity of expression they offer, will continue to attract those who enjoy working directly in clay.

Accessory Cup (detail – view of base), East Lothian, Scotland, *c.*1900–1500 BC, 6.5 cm/h. Incised decoration. © *The Trustees of the National Museums of Scotland 1996 (EC 4).* (See photograph on page 77.)

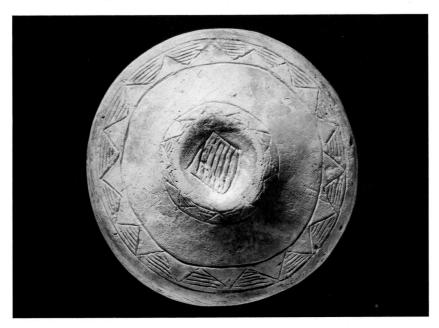

Bibliography

Books

Barley, Nigel, *Smashing Pots – Feats of Clay from Africa*. British Museum Press, 1994.

Blandino, Betty, *Coiled Pottery – Traditional and Contemporary Ways*. A & C Black, 1984.

Bourriau, Janine, *Umm El-Ga'ab – Pottery from the Nile Valley before the Arab Conquest* (Catalogue for an Exhibition at the Fitzwilliam Museum, Cambridge). Cambridge University Press, 1981.

Briscoe, Teresa, 'Anglo-Saxon Pot Stamps', *Anglo-Saxon Studies In Archaeology and History*, **2**, 1981.

Briscoe, Teresa, 'The Use of Brooches and other Jewellery as Dies on Pagan Anglo-Saxon Pottery', *Medieval Archaeology*, **29**, 1985.

Brown, A.C. and Catlin, H.W., *Ancient Cyprus*, Ashmolean Museum, University of Oxford, 1986.

Casson, Michael, *The Craft of the Potter*, British Broadcasting Corporation, 1983.

Clarke D.L., *Beaker Pottery of Great Britain and Ireland* (2 Vols), Cambridge University Press, 1970.

Clarke, D.V., Cowie, T.G. and Foxon, A., *Symbols of Power at the Time of Stonehenge*, HMSO, Edinburgh, 1985.

Elsdon, Sheila M., *Later Prehistoric Pottery*, Shire Archaeology, 1989.

Fitton, J. Lesley, *Cycladic Art*, British Museum Press, 1989.

Gibson, Alex, *Neolithic and Early Bronze Age Pottery*, Shire Archaeology, 1986.

Gibson, Alex and Woods, Ann, *Prehistoric Pottery for the Archaeologist*, Leicester University Press, 1990.

Gibson, John, *Pottery Decoration – Contemporary Approaches*, A & C Black, 1987.

Gompertz, G. St. G. M., *Korean Celadon and Other Wares of the Koryo Period*, Faber and Faber (from the Faber Monographs on Pottery and Porcelain series), 1958.

Gompertz, G. St. G. M., *Korean Pottery and Porcelain of the Yi Period*, Faber and Faber (from the Faber Monographs on Pottery and Porcelain series), 1968.

Goring, Elizabeth, *A Mischievous Pastime – Digging in Cyprus in the Nineteenth Century*, National Museums of Scotland, 1988.

Haslam, Jeremy, *Medieval Pottery*, Shire Archaeology, 1989.

Hennessy, Basil, *Masterpieces of Western and Near Eastern Ceramics. No. 1 Ancient Near Eastern Pottery*, Kodansha, 1979.

Kennett, David H., *Anglo-Saxon Pottery*, Shire Archaeology, 1989.

Kidder, J. Edward, *Prehistoric Japanese Arts – Jomon Pottery*, Kodansha International 1976.

Lacy, A.C., *Greek Pottery in the Bronze Age*, Methuen & Co. Ltd., 1967.

Leigh-Ross, Sylvia, *Nigerian Pottery*, Ibadan University Press, 1970.

Lewis, David, *Warren MacKenzie – An American Potter*, Kodansha, 1991.

Mansfield, Janet, *Salt-glaze Ceramics – An International Perspective*, Craftsman House (Australia) and A & C Black (UK), 1991.

May, Patricia and Tuckson, Margaret, *The Traditional Pottery of Papua New Guinea*, Bay Books, 1982.

McKillop, Beth, *Korean Art and Design – The Samsung Gallery of Korean Art*, Victoria and Albert Museum, 1992.

Medley, Margaret, *The Chinese Potter – A Practical History of Chinese Ceramics*, Phaidon, 1986.

Mikami, Tsugio, *The Art of Japanese Ceramics*, Weatherhill, New York, and Heibonsha, Tokyo, 1976.

Moorey, P.R.S., *Archaeology, Artefacts and the Bible*, Ashmolean Museum, University of Oxford, 1969.

Moorey, P.R.S., *The Ancient Near East*, Ashmolean Museum Publications, University of Oxford, 1987.

Morris, Desmond, *The Art of Ancient Cyprus*, Phaidon Press, 1985.

Rackham, Bernard, *Medieval English Pottery*, Faber and Faber (from the Faber Monographs on Pottery and Porcelain series), 1972.

Rhodes, Daniel, *Clay and Glazes for the Potter*, Chilton (US) and A & C Black (UK), 1975.

Rhodes, Daniel, *Stoneware & Porcelain – the Art of High-fired Pottery*, Pitman Publishing, 1971.

Roy, Christopher, D., *Women's Art in Africa – Woodfired Pottery from Iowa Collections* (Catalogue for an Exhibition, at the University of Iowa Museum of Art), 1991.

Sanders, Herbert H., with the collaboration of Kenkichi Tomimoto, *The World of Japanese Ceramics*, Kodansha International, 1971.

Taylor, John H., *Egypt and Nubia*, British Museum Press, 1991.

Vainker, S.J., *Chinese Pottery and Porcelain – From Prehistory to the Present*, British Museum Press, 1991.

Vandiver, Pamela, in collaboration with Olga Soffer and Bohuslav Klima, 'The Origins of Ceramics: Figurine Manufacture at Dolni Vestonice, circa 26,000 BP (before the present),' *The Studio Potter*, **20**(1), December 1991.

Walker, C.B.F., *Cuneiform* (from the 'Reading the Past' series), British Museum Press, 1993.

Watson, William, *The Genius of China*, (Catalogue of an exhibition held at the Royal Academy, London), 1973.

Whitford, Philip and Wong, Gordon, *Handmade Pottery Tools*, Kodansha International.

Magazines

The Studio Potter, Box 70, Goffstown, New Hampshire 03045, USA (Published semi-annually).

Ceramics Art and Perception, 35 William Street, Paddington, Sydney, NSW 2021, Australia (Published quarterly).

Ceramics Monthly, PO Box 12788, Columbus, Ohio 43212-9933, USA (Published monthly except July and August).

Ceramic Review, 21 Carnaby Street, London W1V 1PH, England, UK (Published bi-monthly).

Index

Note: page numbers in italic refer to illustrations.